SELECTIONS FROM THE SPURGEON
SERMON ARCHIVE

SELECTIONS FROM THE SPURGEON SERMON ARCHIVE

Charles Spurgeon

RELEVANT BOOKS

Published by RELEVANT Books
A division of RELEVANT Media Group, Inc.

www.relevantbooks.com
www.relevantmediagroup.com

© 2006 RELEVANT Media Group

Design by RELEVANT Solutions
Cover design by Ben Pieratt
Interior design by Ben Pieratt, Jeremy Kennedy, Anna Melcon, Aaron Maurer

RELEVANT Books is a registered trademark of RELEVANT Media Group,
Inc., and is registered in the U.S. Patent and Trademark Office.

For information or bulk orders:
RELEVANT MEDIA GROUP, INC.
100 SOUTH LAKE DESTINY DR., STE 200
ORLANDO, FL 32810
407-660-1411

Library of Congress Control Number: 2005911202
International Standard Book Number: 0-9776167-3-8

06 07 08 09 10 8 7 6 5 4 3 2 1

Printed in the United States of America

CONTENTS

INTRODUCTION

There's a famous saying on the British two-pound coin, attributed to Sir Isaac Newton, that goes something like this: if I have seen a little further, it is by "standing on the shoulders of giants." The purpose of this Foundations of Faith series is to introduce you to spiritual giants, one of whom is Charles Haddon Spurgeon. C.H. Spurgeon was the most famous English Baptist preacher of the nineteenth century. His flamboyancy earned him the titles "Prince of Preachers" and the "Preaching Boy Wonder." Today, there is more material in print by Spurgeon than by any other Christian author, living or dead. His heroes were fearless Protestants who were burned to death for their faith and daring Puritans, such as John Bunyan, who were jailed for their convictions. He "stood on their shoulders" and took his impact on the culture around him to a whole new level.

After experiencing a spiritual awakening one night in the middle of a snowstorm, Spurgeon began preaching at the age of sixteen. A year later he became a Baptist pastor. With his vivid and emotionally charged sermons, his influence became so widely respected that he was offered a pastorate at London's famous New Park

Street Chapel. By the time he was twenty, the swelling congregation moved to the Surrey Music Hall, where Spurgeon began preaching to crowds of ten thousand. The congregation moved again, to the Metropolitan Tabernacle—the first modern "megachurch." To give you perspective, think of your kid brother launching a church like Rick Warren's Saddleback in Southern California.

What touches me most about Surgeon's ministry was his ability to speak to the people of the street, common people like you and me. His church became known as a "church of shopkeepers," even amidst much criticism from the evangelically minded. The Established Church and news journals like *The Ipswich Express* described his sermons as "redolent of bad taste, vulgar, and theatrical." But Spurgeon recognized the power of preaching to his generation in their language and in a way that intersected with their daily experiences. Spurgeon replied, "I am perhaps vulgar, but it's not intentional, save that I must and will make the people listen. My firm conviction is that we have had quite enough polite preachers, and many require a change. God has owned me among the most degraded and off-cast. Let others serve their class; these are mine, and to them I must keep."

Living in a highly competitive and materialistic age, we can look to the example of Spurgeon, who understood the snobbery of the upper-middle class's religiosity and its irrelevance to the people around him. He wasn't afraid to speak to people in their own raw and gritty vernacular to pierce them with the importance of the Gospel to their lives. His messages connected with working-class people, tavern maids, housecleaners, farmhands, trash collectors, seamstresses, chimney sweepers, orphans, beggars, and prostitutes. Like Jesus and His disciples, Spurgeon spoke to people where they were and addressed their felt needs: justice for the poor in spirit and hope for the brokenhearted. One newspaper cartoon depicted an Anglican rector driving an old stagecoach with two slow horses named "Church" and "State." Racing ahead was a young preacher with flowing hair, speeding on a train engine. The title: "The Spurgeon." His ministry was provocative but infinitely more powerful and life-changing than the old models.

Devoted to Scripture, disciplined prayer, and godly living, Spurgeon modeled Christian commitment, and this empowered his preaching. But he was human too. Spurgeon's weakness was his health. One scholar wrote, "Perhaps it is correct to say that as a preacher, Spurgeon had everything, except good health. He suffered constantly from various ailments and fell into serious depression at times." Described by his peers as a "moderate Calvinist, warmly evangelistic, liberal in his politics," Spurgeon was extremely ambitious about the kingdom. He wrote many books, edited a magazine, trained future ministers, and had an unquenchable work ethic. All in all, Spurgeon said he had but one solitary purpose: "I take my text and make a beeline to the cross." His single burning desire was to see people come to Jesus Christ, and in his words, "Saving faith is an immediate relation to Christ, accepting, receiving, and resting upon Him alone, for justification, sanctification, and eternal life by virtue of God's grace."

Through deep physical trials, Spurgeon learned a lesson concerning Christian suffering that few are willing to embrace. He shared, "My spirits were sunken so low that I could weep by the hour like a child, and yet I knew not what I wept for." He was convinced that there are moments in our lives when God permits us to experience great affliction. Like Spurgeon, we can enter deeply into the presence of God in times of both great joy and great sorrow. I have found that suffering and personal trials can create tender and open hearts, which infuse power into our daily activities and relationships.

In addition to the Metropolitan Tabernacle, Surgeon opened a college and an orphanage for boys and girls, which continued in London until World War II. Spurgeon's sermons were printed on a weekly basis and enjoyed a high circulation. Before his death in 1892 he had preached nearly 3,600 sermons and published forty-nine volumes of commentaries, sayings, anecdotes, sermon illustrations, and devotions.

Yet with all his attention and success, I am fond of the tenderness with which Spurgeon spoke regarding the role of the Holy Spirit as our Comforter: "Oh! there is a voice in love, it speaks a language which is its own; it has an idiom and a brogue which none can mimic; wisdom cannot imitate it; oratory cannot attain unto it; it is love alone which can reach the mourning heart; love is the only handkerchief which can wipe the mourner's tears away" (Sermon 5, Volume 1). Spurgeon knew people needed to hear from God in their own tongue, not in the elevated speech of the pious and proud. God speaks to us through His Holy Spirit as parents speak to their children or lovers speak to soul mates. It's a language that communicates directly to the heart and seeks to simultaneously soothe and spur on. Spurgeon saw the fatigue, anxiety, and insecurity in people's lives, and he taught them to trust in the One who understood their situation and spoke a message of hope to their hearts about a better place in eternity.

It is said that upon the death of the missionary Dr. David Livingstone, a tattered copy of one of Spurgeon's printed sermons was found among his belongings. A handwritten inscription was detected at the top of the page: "Very good, D.L." He carried it with him during his travels in Africa. It's my hope that you will take this book with you wherever your journey leads you and be carried higher by Spurgeon's giant faith.

Shirin Taber
Author of *Muslims Next Door*

BIOGRAPHY OF CHARLES SPURGEON

Full Name: Charles Haddon Spurgeon

Date of Birth: June 19, 1834 CE

Family Stats: In 1856 Spurgeon married Susannah, by whom he had twin sons, Charles and Thomas.

Lived In: Born in Kelvedon, Essex; first pastored in Cambridgeshire; moved to London at age twenty, where he lived for the rest of his life.

Occupation: British Baptist preacher and writer. Beginning in 1865, he conducted the monthly magazine *The Sword and the Trowel.*

Claim to Fame: England's best-known preacher for most of the second half of the nineteenth century. In 1854, just four years after his conversion, Spurgeon, then only twenty, was called to the pastorate of London's famed New Park Street Chapel, Southwark. Within a few months, his powers as a preacher had made him famous. Spurgeon also established a pastors' college that is still in operation today in South Norwood, England.

Famous Quote: "A little faith will bring your soul to heaven; a great faith will bring heaven to your soul."

Famous Works: *All of Grace, My Sermon Notes, Morning by Morning, Evening by Evening, The Saint and His Saviour*

Died: January 31, 1892, in Mentone (near Nice, France), from ill health he suffered toward the end of his life

Conversion Experience: Spurgeon became a Christian in January 1850, at the age of fifteen. On his way to a scheduled appointment, a snowstorm forced him to take shelter in a Primitive Methodist chapel in Colchester where, in his own words, "God opened my heart to the salvation message." The preacher was reading from Isaiah 45:22.

Miscellaneous Facts: In 1856, a group of nonbelievers shouted "Fire!" while Spurgeon was giving a sermon, sending the congregation into a panic. In the ensuing chaos to escape, several people were crushed to death on the stairs. This event had an enormous impact on Spurgeon, who afterward found himself unable to preach for a period of several weeks.

Spurgeon's preaching was both popular and controversial; some hailed him as a great orator, while others called him awkward and sacrilegious.

THE IMMUTABILITY OF GOD

A SERMON
(No. 1)

Delivered on Sabbath Morning, January 7th, 1855,
by the REV. C. H. Spurgeon
At New Park Street Chapel, Southwark,

"I am the Lord, I change not; therefore ye sons of
Jacob are not consumed."—Malachi 3:6

IT HAS been said by some one that "the proper study
of mankind is man." I will not oppose the idea, but I
believe it is equally true that the proper study of God's
elect is God; the proper study of a Christian is the
Godhead. The highest science, the loftiest speculation,
the mightiest philosophy, which can ever engage the
attention of a child of God, is the name, the nature,
the person, the work, the doings, and the existence
of the great God whom he calls his Father. There is
something exceedingly improving to the mind in a
contemplation of the Divinity. It is a subject so vast, that
all our thoughts are lost in its immensity; so deep, that
our pride is drowned in its infinity. Other subjects we
can compass and grapple with; in them we feel a kind of
self-content, and go our way with the thought, "Behold

I am wise." But when we come to this master-science, finding that our plumb-line cannot sound its depth, and that our eagle eye cannot see its height, we turn away with the thought, that vain man would be wise, but he is like a wild ass's colt; and with the solemn exclamation, "I am but of yesterday, and know nothing." No subject of contemplation will tend more to humble the mind, than thoughts of God. We shall be obliged to feel—

> "Great God, how infinite art thou,
> What worthless worms are we!"

But while the subject *humbles* the mind it also *expands* it. He who often thinks of God, will have a larger mind than the man who simply plods around this narrow globe. He may be a naturalist, boasting of his ability to dissect a beetle, anatomize a fly, or arrange insects and animals in classes with well nigh unutterable names; he may be a geologist, able to discourse of the megatherium and the plesiosaurus, and all kinds of extinct animals; he may imagine that his science, whatever it is, ennobles and enlarges his mind. I dare say it does, but after all, the most excellent study for expanding the soul, is the science of Christ, and him crucified, and the knowledge of the Godhead in the glorious Trinity. Nothing will so enlarge the intellect, nothing so magnify the whole soul of man, as a devout, earnest, continued investigation of the great subject of the Deity. And, whilst humbling and expanding, this subject is eminently *consolatary*. Oh, there is, in contemplating Christ, a balm for every wound; in musing on the Father, there is a quietus for every grief; and in the influence of the Holy Ghost, there is a balsam for every sore. Would you lose your sorrows? Would you drown your cares? Then go, plunge yourself in the Godhead's deepest sea; be lost in his immensity; and you shall come forth as from a couch of rest, refreshed and invigorated. I know nothing which can so comfort the soul; so calm the swelling billows of grief and sorrow; so speak peace to the winds of trial, as a devout musing upon the subject of the Godhead. It is to that subject that I invite you this morning. We shall present you with one view of it,—that is *the immutability of the glorious Jehovah.* "I am," says my text, "Jehovah," (for so it should be translated) "I am Jehovah, I change not: therefore ye sons of Jacob are not consumed."

There are three things this morning. First of all, *an unchanging God*; secondly, *the persons who derive benefit from this glorious attribute,* "the sons of Jacob;" and thirdly, *the benefit they so derive,* they "are not consumed.' We address ourselves to these points.

I. First of all, we have set before us the doctrine of THE IMMUTABILITY OF GOD. "I am God, I change not." Here I shall attempt to expound, or rather to enlarge the thought, and then afterwards to bring a few arguments to prove its truth.

1. I shall offer some exposition of my text, by first saying, that God is Jehovah, and he changes not *in his essence*. We cannot tell you what Godhead is. We do not know what substance that is which we call God. It is an existence, it is a being; but what that is, we know not. However, whatever it is, we call it his essence, and that essence never changes. The substance of mortal things is ever changing. The mountains with their snow-white crowns, doff their old diadems in summer, in rivers trickling down their sides, while the storm cloud gives them another coronation; the ocean, with its mighty floods, loses its water when the sunbeams kiss the waves, and snatch them in mists to heaven; even the sun himself requires fresh fuel from the hand of the Infinite Almighty, to replenish his ever burning furnace. All creatures change. Man, especially as to his body, is always undergoing revolution. Very probably there is not a single particle in my body which was in it a few years ago. This frame has been worn away by activity, its atoms have been removed by friction, fresh particles of matter have in the mean time constantly accrued to my body, and so it has been replenished; but its substance is altered. The fabric of which this world is made is ever passing away; like a stream of water, drops are running away and others are following after, keeping the river still full, but always changing in its elements.

But God is perpetually the same. He is not composed of any substance or material, but is spirit—pure, essential, and ethereal spirit—and therefore he is immutable. He remains everlastingly the same. There are no furrows on his eternal brow. No age hath palsied him; no years have marked him with the mementoes of their flight; he sees ages pass, but with him it is ever *now*. He is the great I AM—the Great Unchangeable. Mark you, his essence did not undergo a change when it became united with the manhood. When Christ in past years did gird himself with mortal clay, the essence of his divinity was not changed; flesh did not become God, nor did God become flesh by a real actual change of nature; the two were united in hypostatical union, but the Godhead was still the same. It was the same when he was a babe in the manger, as it was when he stretched the curtains of heaven; it was the same God that hung upon the cross, and whose blood flowed down in a purple river, the self-same God that holds the world upon his everlasting shoulders, and bears in his hands the keys of death and hell. He never has been changed in his essence, not even by his incarnation; he remains everlastingly, eternally, the one unchanging God, the Father of lights, with whom there is no variableness, neither the shadow of a change.

2. He changes not *in his attributes*. Whatever the attributes of God were of old, that they are now; and of each of

them we may sing "As it was in the beginning, is now, and ever shall be, world without end, Amen." Was he *powerful*? Was he the mighty God when he spake the world out of the womb of nonexistence? Was he the Omnipotent when he piled the mountains and scooped out the hollow places for the rolling deep? Yes, he was powerful then, and his arm is unpalsied now, he is the same giant in his might; the sap of his nourishment is undried, and the strength of his soul stands the same for ever. Was he wise when he constituted this mighty globe, when he laid the foundations of the universe? Had he *wisdom* when he planned the way of our salvation, and when from all eternity he marked out his awful plans? Yes, and he is wise now; he is not less skillful, he has not less knowledge; his eye which seeth all things is undimmed; his ear which heareth all the cries, sighs, sobs, and groans of his people, is not rendered heavy by the years which he hath heard their prayers. He is unchanged in his wisdom, he knows as much now as ever, neither more nor less; he has the same consummate skill, and the same infinite forecastings. He is unchanged, blessed be his name, in his *justice*. just and holy was he in the past; just and holy is he now. He is unchanged in his *truth*; he has promised, and he brings it to pass; he hath saith it, and it shall be done. He varies not in the *goodness*, and generosity, and benevolence of his nature. He is not become an Almighty tyrant, whereas he was once an Almighty Father; but his strong love stands like a

6

granite rock, unmoved by the hurricanes of our iniquity. And blessed be his dear name, he is unchanged in his *love*. When he first wrote the covenant, how full his heart was with affection to his people. He knew that his Son must die to ratify the articles of that agreement. He knew right well that he must rend his best beloved from his bowels, and send him down to earth to bleed and die. He did not hesitate to sign that mighty covenant; nor did he shun its fulfillment. He loves as much now as he did then, and when suns shall cease to shine, and moons to show their feeble light, he still shall love on for ever and for ever. Take any one attribute of God, and I will write *semper idem* on it (always the same). Take any one thing you can say of God now, and it may be said not only in the dark past, but in the bright future it shall always remain the same: "I am Jehovah, I change not."

3. Then again, God changes not in his *plans*. That man began to build, but was not able to finish, and therefore he changed his plan, as every wise man would do in such a case; he built upon a smaller foundation and commenced again. But has it ever been said that God began to build but was not able to finish? Nay. When he hath boundless stores at his command, and when his own right hand would create worlds as numerous as drops of morning dew, shall he ever stay because he has not power? and reverse, or alter, or disarrange his plan, because he cannot carry it out? "But," say some,

"perhaps God never had a plan." Do you think God is more foolish than yourself then, sir? Do you go to work without a plan? "No," say you, "I have always a scheme." So has God. Every man has his plan, and God has a plan too. God is a master-mind; he arranged everything in his gigantic intellect long before he did it; and once having settled it, mark you, he never alters it. "This shall be done," saith he, and the iron hand of destiny marks it down, and it is brought to pass. "This is my purpose," and it stands, nor can earth or hell alter it. "This is my decree," saith he, promulgate it angels; rend it down from the gate of heaven ye devils; but ye cannot alter the decree; it shall be done. God altereth not his plans; why should he? He is Almighty, and therefore can perform his pleasure. Why should he? He is the All-wise, and therefore cannot have planned wrongly. Why should he? He is the everlasting God, and therefore cannot die before his plan is accomplished. Why should he change? Ye worthless atoms of existence, ephemera of the day! Ye creeping insects upon this bayleaf of existence! ye may change *your* plans, but he shall never, never change *his*. Then has he told me that his plan is to save me? If so, I am safe.

> "My name from the palms of his hands
>   Eternity will not erase;
>   Impress'd on his heart it remains,
>   In marks of indelible grace."

4. Yet again, God is unchanging in his *promises*. Ah! we love to speak about the sweet promises of God; but if we could ever suppose that one of them could be changed, we would not talk anything more about them. If I thought that the notes of the bank of England could not be cashed next week, I should decline to take them; and if I thought that God's promises would never be fulfilled—if I thought that God would see it right to alter some word in his promises—farewell Scriptures! I want immutable things: and I find that I have immutable promises when I turn to the Bible: for, "by two immutable things in which it is impossible for God to lie," he hath signed, confirmed, and sealed every promise of his. The gospel is not "yea and nay," it is not promising today, and denying tomorrow; but the gospel is "yea, yea," to the glory of God. Believer! there was a delightful promise which you had yesterday; and this morning when you turned to the Bible the promise was not sweet. Do you know why? Do you think the promise had changed? Ah, no! *You* changed; that is where the matter lies. You had been eating some of the grapes of Sodom, and your mouth was thereby put out of taste, and you could not detect the sweetness. But there was the same honey there, depend upon it, the same preciousness. "Oh!" says one child of God, "I had built my house firmly once upon some stable promises; there came a wind, and I said, O Lord, I am cast down and I shall be lost." Oh! the promises were

not cast down; the foundations were not removed; it was your little "wood, hay, stubble" hut, that you had been building. It was that which fell down. *You* have been shaken *on* the rock, not the rock *under* you. But let me tell you what is the best way of living in the world. I have heard that a gentleman said to a Negro, "I can't think how it is you are always so happy in the Lord and I am often downcast." "Why Massa," said he, "I throw myself flat down on the promise—there I lie; you stand on the promise—you have a little to do with it, and down you go when the wind comes, and then you cry, 'Oh! I am down;' whereas I go flat on the promise at once, and that is why I fear no fall." Then let us always say, "Lord there is the promise; it is thy business to fulfill it." Down I go on the promise flat! no standing up for me. That is where you should go—prostrate on the promise; and remember, every promise is a rock, an unchanging thing. Therefore, at his feet cast yourself, and rest there forever.

5. But now comes one jarring note to spoil the theme. To some of you God is unchanging in his *threatenings*. If every promise stands fast, and every oath of the covenant is fulfilled, hark thee, sinner!—mark the word—hear the death-knell of thy carnal hopes; see the funeral of thy fleshly trustings. Every threatening of God, as well as every promise shall be fulfilled. Talk of decrees! I will tell you of a decree: "He that believeth not shall be

damned." That is a decree, and a statute that can never change. Be as good as you please, be as moral as you can, be as honest as you will, walk as uprightly as you may,—there stands the unchangeable threatening: "He that believeth not shall be damned." What sayest thou to that, moralist? Oh, thou wishest thou couldst alter it, and say, "He that does not live a holy life shall be damned." That will be true; but it does not say so. It says, "He that believeth not." Here is the stone of stumbling, and the rock of offence; but you cannot alter it. You must believe or be damned, saith the Bible; and mark, that threat of God is an unchangeable as God himself. And when a thousand years of hell's torments shall have passed away, you shall look on high, and see written in burning letters of fire, "He that believeth not *shall* be damned." "But, Lord, I *am* damned." Nevertheless it says "*shall be*" still. And when a million ages have rolled away, and you are exhausted by your pains and agonies, you shall turn up your eye and still read "SHALL BE DAMNED," unchanged, unaltered. And when you shall have thought that eternity must have spun out its last thread—that every particle of that which we call eternity, must have run out, you shall still see it written up there, "SHALL BE DAMNED." O terrific thought! How dare I utter it? But I must. Ye must be warned, sirs, "lest ye also come into this place of torment." Ye must be told rough things; for if God's gospel is not a rough thing & the law is a rough thing; Mount Sinai is a rough thing. Woe unto the watchman that warns not the ungodly! God is unchanging in his threatenings. Beware, O sinner, for "it is a fearful thing to fall into the hands of the living God."

6. We must just hint at one thought before we pass away and that is—God is unchanging in the *objects of his love*—not only in his love, but in the *objects* of it.

> "If ever it should come to pass,
> That sheep of Christ might fall away.
> My fickle, feeble soul, alas,
> Would fall a thousand times a day."

If one dear saint of God had perished, so might all; if one of the covenant ones be lost, so may all be, and then there is no gospel promise true; but the Bible is a lie, and there is nothing in it worth my acceptance. I will be an infidel at once, when I can believe that a saint of God can ever fall finally. If God hath loved me once, then he will love me for ever.

> "Did Jesus once upon me shine,
> Then Jesus is for ever mine."

The objects of everlasting love never change. Those whom God hath called, he will justify; whom he has justified, he will sanctify; and whom he sanctifies, he will glorify.

1. Thus having taken a great deal too much time, perhaps, in simply expanding the thought of an unchanging God, I will now try to prove that *He is* unchangeable. I am not much of an argumentative preacher, but one argument that I will mention is this: *the very existence, and being of a God, seem to me to imply immutability.* Let me think a moment. There is a God; this God rules and governs all things; this God fashioned the world: he upholds and maintains it. What kind of being must he be? It does strike me that you cannot think of a changeable God. I conceive that the thought is so repugnant to common sense, that if you for one moment think of a changing God, the words seem to clash, and you are obliged to say, "Then he must be a kind of man," and get a Mormonite idea of God. I imagine it is impossible to conceive of a changing God; it is so to me. Others may be capable of such an idea, but I could not entertain it. I could no more think of a changing God, than I could of a round square, or any other absurdity. The thing seems so contrary, that I am obliged, when once I say God, to include the idea of an unchanging being.

2. Well, I think that one argument will be enough, but another good argument may be found in the fact of *God's perfection.* I believe God to be a perfect being. Now, if he is a perfect being, he cannot change. Do you not see this? Suppose I am perfect today, if it were possible for me to change, should I be perfect tomorrow

after the alteration? If I changed, I must either change from a good state to a better—and then if I could get better, I could not be perfect *now*—or else from a better state to a worse—and if I were worse, I should not be perfect *then*. If I am perfect, I cannot be altered without being imperfect. If I am perfect today, I must keep the same tomorrow if I am to be perfect then. So, if God is perfect, he must be the same; for change would imply imperfection now, or imperfection then.

3. Again, there is the fact of *God's infinity*, which puts change out of the question. God is an infinite being. What do you mean by that? There is no man who can tell you what he means by an infinite being. But there cannot be two infinities. If one thing is infinite, there is no room for anything else; for infinite means all. It means not bounded, not finite, having no end. Well, there cannot be two infinities. If God is infinite today, and then should change and be infinite tomorrow, there would be two infinities. But that cannot be. Suppose he is infinite and then changes, he must become finite, and could not be God; either he is finite today and finite tomorrow, or infinite today and finite tomorrow, or finite today and infinite tomorrow—all of which suppositions are equally absurd. The fact of his being an infinite being at once quashes the thought of his being a changeable being. Infinity has written on its very brow the word "immutability."

4. But then, dear friends, let us look at *the past*: and there we shall gather some proofs of God's immutable nature. "Hath he spoken, and hath he not done it? Hath he sworn, and hath it not come to pass?" Can it not be said of Jehovah, "He hath done all his will, and he hath accomplished all his purpose?" Turn ye to Philistia; ask where she is. God said, "Howl Ashdod, and ye gates of Gaza, for ye shall fall;" and where are they? Where is Edom? Ask Petra and its ruined walls. Will they not echo back the truth that God hath said, "Edom shall be a prey, and shall be destroyed?" Where is Babel, and where Nineveh? Where Moab and where Ammon? Where are the nations God hath said he would destroy? Hath he not uprooted them and cast out the remembrance of them from the earth? And hath God cast off his people? Hath he once been unmindful of his promise? Hath he once broken his oath and covenant, or once departed from his plan? Ah! no. Point to one instance in history where God has changed! Ye cannot, sirs; for throughout all history there stands the fact that God has been immutable in his purposes. Methinks I hear some one say, "I can remember one passage in Scripture where God changed!" And so did I think once. The case I mean, is that of the death of Hezekiah. Isaiah came in and said, 'Hezekiah, you must die, your disease is incurable, set your house in order.' He turned his face to the wall and began to pray; and before Isaiah was in the outer court, he was told to go back and say,

"Thou shalt live fifteen years more." You may think that proves that God changes; but really I cannot see in it the slightest proof in the world. How do you know that God did not know that? Oh! but God did know it; he knew that Hezekiah would live. Then he did not change, for if he knew that, how could he change? That is what I want to know. But do you know one little thing?—that Hezekiah's son Manasseh, was not born at that time, and that had Hezekiah died, there would have been no Manasseh, and no Josiah and no Christ, because Christ came from that very line. You will find that Manasseh was twelve years old when his father died; so that he must have been born three years after this. And do you not believe that God decreed the birth of Manasseh, and foreknew it? Certainly. Then he decreed that Isaiah should go and tell Hezekiah that his disease was incurable, and then say also in the same breath, "But I will cure it, and thou shalt live." He said that to stir up Hezekiah to prayer. He spoke, in the first place as a man. "According to all human probability your disease is incurable, and you must die." Then he waited till Hezekiah prayed; then came a little "but" at the end of the sentence. Isaiah had not finished the sentence. He said, "You must put your house in order for there is no human cure; but" (and then he walked out. Hezekiah prayed a little, and then he came in again, and said) "*But* I will heal thee." Where is there any contradiction there, except in the brain of those who fight against the

Lord, and wish to make him a changeable being.

II. Now secondly, let me say a word on THE PERSONS TO WHOM THIS UNCHANGEABLE GOD IS A BENEFIT. "I am God, I change not; therefore ye sons of Jacob are not consumed." Now, who are "the sons of Jacob," who can rejoice in an immutable God?

1. First, they are the *sons of God's election*; for it is written, "Jacob have I loved, and Esau have I hated, the children being not yet born neither having done good nor evil." It was written, "The elder shall serve the younger." "The sons of Jacob"—

> "Are the sons of God's election,
> Who through sovereign grace believe;
> Be eternal destination
> Grace and glory they receive."

God's elect are here meant by "the sons of Jacob,"—those whom he foreknew and fore-ordained to everlasting salvation.

2. By "the sons of Jacob" are meant, in the second place, *persons who enjoy peculiar rights and titles*. Jacob, you know, had no rights by birth; but he soon acquired them. He changed a mess of pottage with his brother Esau, and thus gained the birthright. I do not justify

the means; but he did also obtain the blessing, and so acquired peculiar rights. By "the sons of Jacob" here, are meant persons who have peculiar rights and titles. Unto them that believe, he hath given the right and power to become sons of God. They have an interest in the blood of Christ; they have a right to "enter in through the gates into the city;" they have a title to eternal honors; they have a promise to everlasting glory; they have a right to call themselves sons of God. Oh! there are peculiar rights and privileges belonging to the "sons of Jacob."

3. But, then next, these "sons of Jacob" were *men of peculiar manifestations*. Jacob had peculiar manifestations from his God, and thus he was highly honored. Once at night-time he lay down and slept; he had the hedges for his curtains, the sky for his canopy, a stone for his pillow, and the earth for his bed. Oh! then he had a peculiar manifestation. There was a ladder, and he saw the angels of God ascending and descending. He thus had a manifestation of Christ Jesus, as the ladder which reaches from earth to heaven, up and down which angels came to bring us mercies. Then what a manifestation there was at Mahanaim, when the angels of God met him; and again at Peniel, when he wrestled with God, and saw him face to face. Those were peculiar manifestations; and this passage refers to those who, like Jacob, have had peculiar manifestations.

Now then, how many of you have had personal manifestations? "Oh!" you say "that is enthusiasm; that is fanaticism." Well, it is a blessed enthusiasm, too, for the sons of Jacob have had peculiar manifestations. They have talked with God as a man talketh with his friend; they have whispered in the ear of Jehovah; Christ hath been with them to sup with them, and they with Christ; and the Holy Spirit hath shone into their souls with such a mighty radiance, that they could not doubt about special manifestations. The "sons of Jacob" are the men, who enjoy these manifestations.

4. Then again, they are *men of peculiar trials*. Ah! poor Jacob! I should not choose Jacob's lot if I had not the prospect of Jacob's blessing; for a hard lot his was. He had to run away from his father's house to Laban's; and then that surly old Laban cheated him all the years he was there—cheated him of his wife, cheated him in his wages, cheated him in his flocks, and cheated him all through the story. By-and-bye he had to run away from Laban, who pursued him and overtook him. Next came Esau with four hundred men to cut him up root and branch. Then there was a season of prayer, and afterwards he wrestled, and had to go all his life with his thigh out of joint. But a little further on, Rachael, his dear beloved, died. Then his daughter Dinah is led astray, and the sons murder the Shechemites. Anon there is dear Joseph sold into Egypt, and a famine comes. Then Reuben goes

up to his couch and pollutes it; Judah commits incest with his own daughter-in-law; and all his sons become a plague to him. At last Benjamin is taken away; and the old man, almost broken-hearted, cries, "Joseph is not, and Simeon is not, and ye will take Benjamin away." Never was man more tried than Jacob, all through the one sin of cheating his brother. All through his life God chastised him. But I believe there are many who can sympathize with dear old Jacob. They have had to pass through trials very much like his. Well, cross-bearers! God says, "I change not; therefore ye sons of Jacob are not consumed." Poor tried souls! ye are not consumed because of the unchanging nature of your God. Now do not get fretting, and say, with the self-conceit of misery, "I am the man who hath seen affliction." Why "the Man of Sorrows" was afflicted more than you; Jesus was indeed a mourner. You only see the skirts of the garments of affliction. You never have trials like his. You do not understand what troubles means; you have hardly sipped the cup of trouble; you have only had a drop or two, but Jesus drunk the dregs. Fear not saith God, "I am the Lord, I change not; therefore ye sons of Jacob," men of peculiar trials, "are not consumed."

5. Then one more thought about who are the "sons of Jacob," for I should like you to find out whether you are "sons of Jacob," yourselves. They are *men of peculiar character*, for though there were some things about Jacob's

character which we cannot commend, there are one or two things which God commends. There was Jacob's faith, by which Jacob had his name written amongst the mighty worthies who obtained not the promises on earth, but shall obtain them in heaven. Are you men of faith, beloved? Do you know what it is to walk by faith, to live by faith, to get your temporary food by faith, to live on spiritual manna—all by faith? Is faith the rule of your life? if so, you are the "sons of Jacob."

Then Jacob was a man of *prayer*—a man who wrestled, and groaned, and prayed. There is a man up yonder who never prayed this morning, before coming up to the house of God. Ah! you poor heathen, don't you pray? No! he says, "I never thought of such a thing; for years I have not prayed." Well, I hope you may before you die. Live and die without prayer, and you will pray long enough when you get to hell. There is a woman: she did not pray this morning; she was so busy sending her children to the Sunday School, she had no time to pray. No time to pray? Had you time to dress? There is a time for every purpose under heaven, and if you had purposed to pray, you would have prayed. Sons of God cannot live without prayer. They are wrestling Jacobs. They are men in whom the Holy Ghost so works, they they can no more live without prayer than I can live without breathing. They must pray. Sirs, mark you, if you are living without prayer, you are living without

Christ; and dying like that, your portion will be in the lake which burneth with fire. God redeem you, God rescue you from such a lot! But you who are "the sons of Jacob," take comfort, for God is immutable.

III. Thirdly, I can say only a word about the other point—THE BENEFIT WHICH THESE "SONS OF JACOB" RECEIVE FROM AN UNCHANGING GOD. "Therefore ye sons Jacob are not consumed." "Consumed?" How? how can man be consumed? Why, there are two ways. We might have been consumed in hell. If God had been a changing God, the "sons of Jacob" here this morning, might have been consumed *in hell*; but for God's unchanging love I should have been a faggot in the fire. But there is a way of being consumed *in this world*; there is such a things as being condemned before you die—"condemned already;" there is such a thing as being alive, and yet being absolutely dead. We might have been left to our own devices, and then where should we have been now? Revelling with the drunkard, blaspheming Almighty God. Oh? had he left you, dearly beloved, had he been a changing God, ye had been amongst the filthiest of the filthy, and the vilest of the vile. Cannot you remember in your life, seasons similar to those I have felt? I have gone right to the edge of sin; some strong temptation has taken hold of both my arms, so that I could not wrestle with it. I have been pushed alone, dragged as by an awful satanic power to the very edge of some horrid precipice. I have looked down, down, down, and seen my portion; I quivered on the brink of ruin. I have been horrified, as, with my hair upright, I have thought of the sin I was about to commit, the horrible pit into which I was about to fall. A strong arm hath saved me. I have started back and cried, O God! could I have gone so near sin, and yet come back again? Could I have walked right up to the furnace and not fallen down, like Nebuchadnezzar's strong men, devoured by the very heat? Oh! is it possible I should be here this morning, when I think of the sins I have committed, and the crimes which have crossed my wicked imagination? Yes, I am here, unconsumed, because the Lord changes not. Oh! if he had changed, we should have been consumed in a dozen ways; if the Lord had changed, you and I should have been consumed by ourselves; for after all, Mr. Self is the worst enemy a Christian has. We should have proved suicides to our own souls; we should have mixed the cup of poison for our own spirits, if the Lord had not been an unchanging God, and dashed the cup out of our hands when we were about to drink it. Then we should have been consumed by God himself if he had not been a changeless God. We call God a Father; but there is not a father in this world who would not have killed all his children long ago, so provoked would he have been with them, if he had been half as much troubled as God has been with his family. He has the most troublesome family in the whole world—unbelieving, ungrateful, disobedient, forgetful, rebellious, wandering, murmuring, and stiffnecked. Well it is that he is longsuffering, or else he would have taken not only the rod, but the sword to some of us long ago. But there was nothing in us to love at first, so, there cannot be less now. John Newton used to tell a whimsical story, and laugh at it too, of a good woman who said, in order to prove the doctrine of Election, "Ah! sir, the Lord must have loved me before I was born, or else he would not have seen anything in me to love afterwards." I am sure it is true in my case, and true in respect most of God's people; for there is little to love in them after they are born, that if he had not loved them before then, he would have seen no reason to choose them after; but since he loved them without works, he loves them without works still; since their good works did not win his affection, bad works cannot sever that affection; since their righteousness did not bind his love to them, so their wickedness cannot snap the golden links. He loved them out of pure sovereign grace, and he will love them still. But we should have been consumed by the devil, and by our enemies—consumed by the world, consumed by our sins, by our trials, and in a hundred other ways, if God had ever changed.

Well, now, time fails us, and I can say but little. I have

only just cursorily touched on the text. I now hand it to you. May the Lord help you "sons of Jacob" to take home this portion of meat; digest it well, and feed upon it. May the Holy Ghost sweetly apply the glorious things that are written! And may you have "a feast of fat things, of wines on the lees well refined!" Remember God is the same, whatever is removed. Your friends may be disaffected, your ministers may be taken away, every thing may change, but God does not. Your brethren may change and cast out your name as vile: but God will love you still. Let your station in life change, and your property be gone; let your whole life be shaken, and you become weak and sickly; let everything flee away—there is one place where change cannot put his finger; there is one name on which mutability can never be written; there is one heart which never can alter; that heart is God's—that name Love.

> "Trust him, he will ne'er deceive you.
> Though you hardly of him deem;
> He will never, never leave you,
> Nor will let you quite leave him."

THE REMEMBRANCE OF CHRIST

A SERMON
(No. 2)

Delivered on Sabbath Evening, January 7th, 1855,
by the REV. C. H. Spurgeon
At New Park Street Chapel, Southwark,

"This do in remembrance of me."
—1 Corinthians 11:24.

IT SEEMS, then, that Christians may forget Christ. The text implies the possibility of forgetfulness concerning him whom gratitude and affection should constrain them to remember. There could be no need for this loving exhortation, if there were not a fearful supposition that our memories might prove treacherous, and our remembrance superficial in its character, or changing in its nature. Nor is this a bare supposition: it is, alas, too well confirmed in our experience, not as a possibility, but as a lamentable fact. It seems at first sight too gross a crime to lay at the door of converted men. It appears almost impossible that those who have been redeemed by the blood of the dying Lamb should ever forget their Ransomer; that those who have been loved with an everlasting love by the eternal Son of God, should ever forget that Son; but if startling to the ear, it is alas, too apparent to the eye to allow us to deny the fact. Forget him who ne'er forgot us! Forget him who poured his blood forth for our sins! Forget him who loved us even to the death! Can it be possible? Yes it is not only possible, but conscience confesses that it is too sadly a fault of all of us, that we can remember anything except Christ. The object which we should make the monarch of our hearts, is the very thing we are most inclined to forget. Where one would think that memory would linger, and unmindfulness would be an unknown intruder, that is the spot which is desecrated by the feet of forgetfulness, and that the place where memory too seldom looks. I appeal to the conscience of every Christian here: Can you deny the truth of what I utter? Do you not find yourselves forgetful of Jesus? Some creature steals away your heart, and you are unmindful of him upon whom your affection ought to be set. Some earthly business engrosses your attention when you should have your eye steadily fixed upon the cross. It is the incessant round of world, world, world; the constant din of earth, earth, earth, that takes away the soul from Christ. Oh! my friends, is it not too sadly true that we can recollect anything but Christ, and forget nothing so easy as him whom we ought to remember? While memory will preserve a poisoned weed, it suffereth the Rose of Sharon to wither.

The cause of this is very apparent: it lies in one or two facts. We forget Christ, because regenerate persons as we really are, still corruption and death remain even in the regenerate. We forget him because we carry about with us the old Adam of sin and death. If we were purely new-born creatures, we should never forget the name of him whom we love. If we were entirely regenerated beings, we should sit down and meditate on all our Saviour did and suffered; all he is; all he has gloriously promised to perform; and never would our roving affections stray; but centered, nailed, fixed eternally to one object, we should continually contemplate the death and sufferings of our Lord. But alas! we have a worm in the heart, a pest-house, a charnel-house within, lusts, vile imaginations, and strong evil passions, which, like wells of poisonous water, send out continually streams of impurity. I have a heart, which God knoweth, I wish I could wring from my body and hurl to an infinite distance; a soul which is a cage of unclean birds, a den of loathsome creatures, where dragons haunt and owls do congregate, where every evil beast of ill-omen dwells; a heart too vile to have a parallel—"deceitful above all things and desperately wicked." This is the reason why I am forgetful of Christ. Nor is this the sole cause; I suspect it lies somewhere else too. We forget Christ because there are so many other things around us to attract our attention. "But," you say, "they ought not to do so, because though they are around us, they are nothing in comparison with Jesus Christ: though they are in dread proximity to our hearts, what are they compared with Christ?" But do you know, dear friends, that the nearness of an object has a very great effect upon its power? The sun is many, many times larger than the moon, but the moon has a greater influence upon the tides of the ocean than the sun, simply because it is nearer, and has a greater power of attraction. So I find that a little crawling worm of the earth has more effect upon my soul than the glorious Christ in heaven; a handful of golden earth, a puff of fame, a shout of applause, a thriving business, my house, my home, will affect me more than all the glories of the upper world; yea, than the beatific vision itself: simply because earth is near, and heaven is far away. Happy day, when I shall be borne aloft on angels' wings to dwell for ever near my Lord, to bask in the sunshine of his smile, and to be lost in the ineffable radiance of his lovely countenance. We see then the cause of forgetfulness; let us blush over it; let us be sad that we neglect our Lord so much, and now let us attend to his word, "This do in remembrance of me," hoping that its solemn sounds may charm away the demon of base ingratitude.

We shall speak, first of all, concerning *the blessed object of memory*; secondly, upon *the advantages to be derived from remembering this Person*; thirdly, the *gracious help, to our memory*—"This do in *remembrance* of me;" and fourthly,

the *gentle command*, " *This do* in remembrance of me."
May the Holy Ghost open my lips and your hearts, that
we may receive blessings.

I. First of all, we shall speak of THE GLORIOUS AND
PRECIOUS OBJECT OF MEMORY—"This do in
remembrance of *ME*." Christians have many treasures
to lock up in the cabinet of memory. They ought to
remember their *election*—"Chosen of God ere time
began." They ought to be mindful of their *extraction*,
that they were taken out of the miry clay, hewn out of
the horrible pit. They ought to recollect their *effectual
calling*, for they were called of God, and rescued by the
power of the Holy Ghost. They ought to remember
their *special deliverances*—all that has been done for them,
and all the mercies bestowed on them. But there is one
whom they should embalm in their souls with the most
costly spices—one who, above all other gifts of God,
deserves to be had in perpetual remembrance. *One* I
said, for I mean not an act, I mean not a deed; but it
is a Person whose portrait I would frame in gold, and
hang up in the state-room of the soul. I would have
you earnest students of all the *deeds* of the conquering
Messiah. I would have you conversant with the *life* of
our Beloved. But O forget not his *person*; for the text
says, "This do in remembrance of me." It is Christ's
glorious person which ought to be the object of our
remembrance. It is his image which should be enshrined

in every temple of the Holy Ghost.

But some will say, "How can we remember Christ's person, when we never saw it? We cannot tell what was the peculiar form of his visage; we believe his countenance to be fairer than that of any other man—although through grief and suffering more marred—but since we did not see it, we cannot remember it. We never saw his feet as they trod the journeys of his mercy; we never beheld his hands as he stretched them out full of lovingkindness; we cannot remember the wondrous intonation of his language, when in more than seraphic eloquence, he awed the multitude, and chained their ears to him; we cannot picture the sweet smile that ever hung on his lips, nor that awful frown with which he dealt out anathemas against the Pharisees; we cannot remember him in his sufferings and agonies, for we never saw him." Well, beloved, I suppose it is true that you cannot remember the visible appearance, for you were not then born; but do you not know that even the apostle said, though he had known Christ after the flesh, yet, thenceforth after the flesh he would know Christ no more. The natural appearance, the race, the descent, the poverty, the humble garb, were nothing in the apostle's estimation of his glorified Lord. And thus, though you do not know him after the flesh, you may know him after the spirit; in this manner you can remember Jesus as much now as Peter, or Paul, or John, or James, or any of those favoured ones who once trod in his footsteps, walked side by side with him, or laid their heads upon his bosom. Memory annihilates distance and over leapeth time, and can behold the Lord, though he be exalted in glory.

Ah! let us spend five minutes in remembering Jesus. Let us remember him in his *baptism*, when descending into the waters of Jordan, a voice was heard, saying, "This is my beloved Son, in whom I am well pleased." Behold him coming up dripping from the stream! Surely the conscious water must have blushed that it contained its God. He slept within its waves a moment, to consecrate the tomb of baptism, in which those who are dead with Christ are buried with him. Let us remember him in the *wilderness*, whither he went straight from his immersion. Oh! I have often thought of that scene in the desert, when Christ, weary and way-worn, sat him down, perhaps upon the gnarled roots of some old tree. Forty days that he fasted, he was an hungered, when in the extremity of his weakness there came the evil spirit. Perhaps he had veiled his demon royalty in the form of some aged pilgrim, and taking up a stone, said, "Way-worn pilgrim, if thou be the Son of God command this stone to be made bread." Methinks I see him, with his cunning smile, and his malicious leer, as he held the stone, and said, "If,"—blasphemous if,—"If thou be the Son of God, command that this stone shall become a meal for me and thee, for both of us are hungry, and it will be an act of mercy; thou canst do it easily; speak the word, and it shall be like the bread of heaven; we will feed upon it, and thou and I will be friends for ever." But Jesus said—and O how sweetly did he say it—"Man shall not live by bread alone." Oh! how wonderfully did Christ fight the tempter! Never was there such a battle as that. It was a duel foot to foot—a single-handed combat—when the champion lion of the pit, and the mighty lion of the tribe of Judah, fought together. Splendid sight! Angels stood around to gaze upon the spectacle, just as men of old did sit to see the tournament of noted warriors. There Satan gathered up his strength; here Apollyon concentrated all his satanic power, that in this giant wrestle he might overthrow the seed of the woman. But Jesus was more than a match for him; in the wrestling he gave him a deadly fall, and came off more than a conqueror. Lamb of God! I will remember thy desert strivings, when next I combat with Satan. When next I have a conflict with roaring Diabolus, I will look to him who conquered once for all, and broke the dragon's head with his mighty blows.

Further, I beseech you remember him in all *his daily temptations* and hourly trials, in that life-long struggle of his, through which he passed. Oh! what a mighty tragedy was the death of Christ! and his life too? Ushered in with a song, it closed with a shriek. "It is finished." It began in a manger, and ended on a cross; but oh, the sad interval between! Oh! the black pictures of persecution, when his friends abhorred him; when his foes frowned at him as he passed the streets; when he heard the hiss of calumny, and was bitten by the foul tooth of envy; when slander said he had a devil and was mad: that he was a drunken man and a wine-bibber; and when his righteous soul was vexed with the ways of the wicked. Oh! Son of God, I must remember thee; I cannot help remembering thee, when I think of those years of toil and trouble which thou didst live for my sake. But you know my chosen theme—the place where I can always best remember Christ. It is a shady garden full of olives. O that spot! I would that I had eloquence, that I might take you there. Oh! if the Spirit would but take us, and set us down hard by the mountains of Jerusalem, I would say, see there runs the brook of Kedron, which the king himself did pass; and there you see the olive trees. Possibly, at the foot of that olive, lay the three disciples when they slept; and there, ah! there, I see drops of blood. Stand here, my soul, a moment; those drops of blood—dost thou behold them? Mark them; they are not the blood of wounds; they are the blood of a man whose body was then unwounded. O my soul picture him when he knelt down in agony and sweat,—sweat, because he wrestled with God,—sweat, because he agonized with his Father. "My Father, if it be possible, let this cup pass from me." O Gethsemane!

thy shades are deeply solemn to my soul. But ah! those drops of blood! Surely it is the climax of the height of misery; it is the last of the mighty acts of this wondrous sacrifice. Can love go deeper than that? Can it stoop to greater deeds of mercy? Oh! had I eloquence, I would bestow a tongue on every drop of blood that is there; that your hearts might rise in mutiny against your languor and coldness, and speak out with earnest burning remembrance of Jesus. And now, farewell, Gethsemane.

But I will take you somewhere else, where you shall still behold the "Man of Sorrows." I will lead you to Pilate's hall, and let you see him endure the mockeries of cruel soldiers: the smitings of mailed gloves; the blows of clenched fists; the shame; the spitting, the plucking of the hair: the cruel buffetings. Oh! can you not picture the King of Martyrs, stript of his garments; exposed to the gaze of fiend-like men? See you not the crown about his temples, each thorn acting as a lancet to pierce his head? Mark you not his lacerated shoulders, and the white bones starting out from the bleeding flesh? Oh, Son of Man! I see thee scourged and flagellated with rods and whips, how can I henceforward cease to remember thee? My memory would be more treacherous than Pilate, did it not every cry, *Ecce Homo*,—"Behold the man."

Now, finish the scene of woe by a view of Calvary.

Think of the pierced hands and the bleeding side; think of the scorching sun, and then the entire darkness; remember the broiling fever and the dread thirst; think of the death shriek, "It is finished!" and of the groans which were its prelude. This is the object of memory. Let us never forget Christ. I beseech you, for the love of Jesus, let him have the chief place in your memories. Let not the pearl of great price be dropped from your careless hand into the dark ocean of oblivion.

I cannot, however, help saying one thing before I leave this head: and that is, there are some of you who can very well carry away what I have said, because you have read it often, and heard it before; but still you cannot spiritually remember anything about Christ, because you never had him manifested to you, and what we have never known, we cannot remember. Thanks be unto God, I speak not of you all, for in this place there is a goodly remnant according to the election of grace, and to them I turn. Perhaps I could tell you of some old barn, hedge-row, or cottage; or if you have lived in London, about some garret, or some dark lane or street, where first you met with Christ; or some chapel into which you strayed, and you might say, "Thank God, I can remember the seat where first he met with me, and spoke the whispers of love to my soul, and told me he had purchased me."

"Dost mind the place, the spot of ground,
Where Jesus did thee meet?"

Yes, and I would love to build a temple on the spot, and to raise some monument there, where Jehovah-Jesus first spoke to my soul, and manifested himself to me. But he has revealed himself to you more than once—has he not? And you can remember scores of places where the Lord hath appeared of old unto you, saying, "Behold I have loved you with an everlasting love." If you cannot all remember such things, there are some of you that can; and I am sure they will understand me when I say, come and do this in remembrance of Christ—in remembrance of all his loving visitations, of his sweet wooing words, of his winning smiles upon you, of all he has said and communicated to your souls. Remember all these things tonight, if it be possible for memory to gather up the mighty aggregate of grace. "Bless the Lord. O my soul, and forget not all his benefits."

II. Having spoken upon the blessed object of our memory, we say, secondly, a little upon THE BENEFITS TO BE DERIVED FROM A LOVING REMEMBRANCE OF CHRIST.

Love never says, *"Cui bono?"* Love never asks what benefit it will derive from love. Love from its very nature is a disinterested thing. It loves; for the creature's sake it loves, and for nothing else. The Christian needs no argument to make him love Christ; just as a mother needs no argument to make her love her child. She does it because it is her nature to do so. The new-born creature must love Christ, it cannot help it. Oh! who can resist the matchless charms of Jesus Christ?—the fairest of ten thousand fairs, the loveliest of ten thousand loves. Who can refuse to adore the prince of perfection, the mirror of beauty, the majestic Son of God? But yet it may be useful to us to observe the advantages of remembering Christ, for they are neither few nor small.

And first, remembrance of Jesus will tend to give you *hope when you are under the burden of your sins*. Notice a few characters here tonight. There comes in a poor creature. Look at him! He has neglected himself this last month; he looks as if he had hardly eaten his daily bread. What is the matter with you? "Oh!" says he, "I have been under a sense of guilt; I have been again and again lamenting, because I fear I can never be forgiven; once I thought I was good, but I have been reading the Bible, and I find that my heart is 'deceitful above all things, and desperately wicked;' I have tried to reform, but the more I try, the deeper I sink in the mire, there is certainly no hope for me. I feel that I deserve no mercy; it seems to me that God must destroy me, for he has declared, 'The soul that sinneth it shall die;' and die I must, be damned I must, for I know I have broken

God's law." How will you comfort such a man? What soft words will you utter to give him peace? *I* know! I will tell thee that there is one, who for thee hath made a complete atonement; if thou only believest on him thou art safe for ever. Remember him, thou poor dying, hopeless creature, and thou shalt be made to sing for joy and gladness. See, the man believes, and in ecstasy exclaims, "Oh! come all ye that fear God, and I will tell you what he hath done for my soul."

"Tell it unto sinners, tell, I am, I am out of hell."

Hallelujah! God hath blotted out my sins like a thick cloud! That is one benefit to be derived from remembering Christ. It gives us hope under a sense of sin, and tells us there is mercy yet.

Now, I must have another character. And what does he say? "I cannot stand it any longer; I have been persecuted and ill-treated, because I love Christ; I am mocked, and laughed at, and despised: I try to bear it, but I really cannot. A man will be a man; tread upon a worm and he will turn upon you; my patience altogether fails me; I am in such a peculiar position that it is of no use to advise me to have patience, for patience I cannot have; my enemies are slandering me, and I do not know what to do." What shall we say to that poor man? How shall we give him patience? What shall we preach to him?

You have heard what he has to say about himself. How shall we comfort him under this great trial? If we suffered the same, what should we wish some friend to say to us? Shall we tell him that other persons have borne as much? He will say, "Miserable comforters are ye all!" No, I will tell him, "Brother, you are persecuted; but remember the words of Jesus Christ, how he spake unto us, and said, 'Rejoice in that day, and leap for joy, for great is your reward in heaven, for so persecuted they the prophets that were before you." My brother! think of him, who, when he died, prayed for his murderers, and said, "Father, forgive them, for they know not what they do." All you have to bear, is as nothing compared with his mighty sufferings. Take courage; face it again like a man; never say die. Let not your patience be gone; take up your cross daily, and follow Christ. Let him be your motto; set him before your eyes. And, now, receiving this, hear what the man will say. He tells you at once—"Hail, persecution; welcome shame. Disgrace for Jesus shall be my honor, and scorn shall be my highest glory.

> "'Now, for the love I bear his name,
> What was my gain I count my loss,
> I pour contempt on all my shame,
> And nail my glory to his cross.'"

There is another effect, you see, to remembering Christ.

It tends to give us *patience under persecution*. It is a girdle to brace up the loins, so that our faith may endure to the end.

Dear friends, I should occupy your time too much if I went into the several benefits; so I will only just run over one or two blessings to be received. It will give us *strength in temptation*. I believe that there are hours with every man, when he has a season of terrific temptation. There was never a vessel that lived upon the mighty deep but sometimes it had to do battle with a storm. There she is, the poor barque, rocked up and down on the mad waves. See how they throw her from wave to wave, and toss her to mid heaven. The winds laugh her to scorn. Old Ocean takes the ship in his dripping fingers, and shakes it to and fro. How the mariners cry out for fear! Do you know how you can put oil upon the waters, and all shall be still? Yes. One potent word shall do it. Let Jesus come; let the poor heart remember Jesus, and steadily then the ship shall sail, for Christ has the helm. The winds shall blow no more, for Christ shall bid them shut their mighty mouths, and never again disturb his child. There is nothing which can give you strength in temptation, and help you to weather the storm, like the name of Jesus Christ, the incarnate Son of God. Then again, what *comfort* it will give you on a sick bed—the name of Christ! It will help you to be patient to those who wait upon you, and to endure the sufferings which you have to bear; yea, it shall be so with you, that you shall have more hope in sickness than in health, and shall find a blessed sweetness in the bitterness of gall. Instead of feeling vinegar in your mouth, through your trouble, you shall find honey for sweetness, in the midst of all the trial and trouble that God will put upon you, "For *he* giveth songs in the night."

But just to close up the advantages of remembering Christ, do you know where you will have the benefit most of all? Do you know the place where chiefly you will rejoice that you ever thought of him? I will take you to it. Hush! Silence! You are going up stairs into a lonely room. The curtains hang down. Some one stands there weeping. Children are around the bed, and friends are there. See that man lying? That is yourself. Look at him; his eyes are your eyes; his hands are your hands. That is yourself. You will be there soon. Man! that is yourself. Do you see it? It is a picture of yourself. Those are your eyes that soon will be closed in death—your hands, that will lie stiff and motionless—your lips that will be dry and parched, between which they will put drops of water. Those are your words that freeze in air, and drop so slowly from your dying lips. I wonder whether you will be able to remember Christ there. If you do not, I will picture you. Behold that man, straight up in the bed; see his eyes starting from their sockets. His friends are all alarmed; they ask him what he sees.

He represses the emotion; he tells them he sees nothing. They know that there is something before his eyes. He starts again. Good God! what is that I see—I seem to see? What is it? Ah! one sigh! The soul is gone. The body is there. What did he see? He saw a flaming throne of judgment; he saw God upon it, with his sceptre; he saw books opened; he beheld the throne of God, and saw a messenger, with a sword brandished in the air to smite him low. Man! that is thyself; there thou wilt be soon. That picture is thine own portrait. I have photographed thee to the life. Look at it. That is where thou shalt be within a few years—ay, within a few days. But if thou canst remember Christ, shall I tell thee what thou wilt do? Oh! thou wilt smile in the midst of trouble. Let me picture such a man. They put pillows behind him; he sits up in bed, and takes the hand of the loved one, and says, "Farewell! weep not for me; the kind God shall wipe away all tears from every eye." Those round about are addressed, "Prepare to meet your God, and follow me to the land of bliss." Now he has set his house in order. All is done. Behold him, like good old Jacob, leaning on his staff, about to die. See how his eyes sparkle; he claps his hands; they gather round to hear what he has to say; he whispers "Victory!" and summoning a little more strength, he cries, "Victory!" and at last, with his final gasp, "Victory, through him that loved us!" and he dies. This is one of the great benefits to be derived from remembering Christ—to be enabled to meet death with blessed composure.

III. We are now arrived at the third portion of our meditation, which is a SWEET AID TO MEMORY.

At schools we used certain books, called "Aids to Memory." I am sure they rather perplexed than assisted me. Their utility was equivalent to that of a bundle of staves under a traveller's arm: true he might use them one by one to walk with, but in the mean time he carried a host of others which he would never need. But our Saviour was wiser than all our teachers, and his remembrances are true and real aids to memory. His love tokens have an unmistakeable language, and they sweetly win our attention.

Behold the whole mystery of the sacred Eucharist. It is bread and wine which are lively emblems of the body and blood of Jesus. The power to excite remembrance consists in *the appeal thus made to the senses*. Here the eye, the hand, the mouth, find joyful work. The bread is tasted, and entering within, works upon the sense of taste, which is one of the most powerful. The wine is sipped—the act is palpable. We know that we are drinking, and thus the senses, which are usually clogs to the soul, become wings to lift the mind in contemplation. Again, much of the influence of this ordinance is found in its simplicity. How beautifully simple the ceremony is—bread broken and wine poured out. There is no calling that thing a chalice, that thing a paten, and that a host. Here is nothing to burden the memory—here is the simple bread and wine. He must have no memory at all who cannot remember that he has eaten bread, and that he has been drinking wine. Note again, the *mighty pregnancy* of these signs—how full they are of meaning. Bread broken—so was your Saviour broken. Bread to be eaten—so his flesh is meat indeed. Wine poured out, the pressed juice of the grape—so was your Saviour crushed under the foot of divine justice: his blood is your sweetest wine. Wine to cheer your heart—so does the blood of Jesus. Wine to strengthen and invigorate you—so does the blood of the mighty sacrifice. Oh! make that bread and wine to your souls tonight a sweet and blessed help of remembrance of that dear Man who once on Calvary died. Like the little ewe lamb, you are now to eat your Master's bread and drink from his cup. Remember the hand which feeds you.

But before you can remember Christ well here, you must ask the assistance of the Holy Spirit. I believe there ought to be a preparation before the Lord's Supper. I do not believe in Mrs. Toogood's preparation, who spent a week in preparing, and then finding it was not the Ordinance Sunday, she said she had lost all the week. I do not believe in that kind of preparation, but I do believe in a holy preparation for the Lord's Supper: when we can on a Saturday if possible, spend an hour in quiet meditation on Christ, and the passion of Jesus;

when, especially on the Sabbath afternoon, we can devoutly sit down and behold him, then these scenes become realities, and not mockeries, as they are to some. I fear greatly that there are some of you who will drink the wine, and not think of his blood: and vile hypocrites you will be while you do it. Take heed to yourselves, "He that eateth and drinketh" unworthily, eateth and drinketh—what?—"damnation to himself." This is a plain English word; mind what you are doing! Do not do it carelessly; for of all the sacred things on earth, it is the most solemn. We have heard of some men banded together by drawing blood from their arms and drinking it all round; that was most horrid, but at the same time most solemn. Here you are to drink blood from the veins of Christ, and sip the trickling stream which gushed from his own loving heart. Is not that a solemn thing? Ought anybody to trifle with it? To go to church and take it for sixpence? To come and join us for the sake of getting charities? Out upon it! It is an awful blasphemy against Almighty God; and amongst the damned in hell, those shall be among the most accursed who dared thus to mock the holy ordinance of God. This is the remembrance of Christ. "This do in remembrance of me." If you cannot do it in remembrance of Christ, I beseech you, as you love your souls, do not do it at all. Oh! regenerate man or woman, enter not into the court of the priests, lest Israel's God resent the intrusion.

IV. And now to close up. Here is a sweet command: "This do in remembrance of me." To whom does this command apply? "This do ye." It is important to answer this question—"This do ye," Who are intended? *Ye who put your trust in me.* "This do ye in remembrance of me." Well, now, you should suppose Christ speaking to you tonight; and he says, "This do ye in remembrance of me." Christ watches you at the door. Some of you go home, and Christ says, "I thought I said, 'This do ye in remembrance of me.'" Some of you keep your seats as spectators. Christ sits with you, and he says, "I thought I said, 'This do ye in remembrance of me.'" "Lord, I know you did." "Do you love me then?" "Yes, I love thee; I love, Lord; thou knowest I do." "But, I say, go down there—eat that bread, drink that wine." "I do not like to, Lord; I should have to be baptized if I joined that church, and I am afraid I shall catch cold, or be looked at. I am afraid to go before the church, for I think they would ask some questions I could not answer." "What," says Christ, "is this all you love me? Is this all your affection to your Lord. Oh! how cold to me, your Saviour. If I had loved you no more than this, you would have been in hell: if that were the full extent of my affection, I should not have died for you. Great love bore great agonies; and is this all your gratitude to me?" Are not some of you ashamed, after this? Do you not say in your hearts, "it is really wrong?" Christ says, "Do this in remembrance of me," and are you not ashamed to stay away? I give a free invitation to every lover of Jesus to come to this table. I beseech you, deny not yourselves the privilege by refusing to unite with the church. If you still live in sinful neglect of this ordinance, let me remind you that Christ has said, "Whosoever shall be ashamed of me in this generation, of him will I be ashamed, when I come in the glory of my Father." Oh, soldier of the cross, act not the coward's part!

And not to lead you into any mistakes, I must just add one thing, and then I have done. When I speak of your taking the ordinance of the Lord's Supper, do not imagine that I wish you for one moment to suppose that there is anything saving in it. Some say that the ordinance of baptism is non-essential, so is the ordinance of the Lord's Supper, it is non-essential, if we look upon it in the light of salvation. Be saved by eating a piece of bread! Nonsense, confounded nonsense! Be saved by drinking a drop of wine! Why, it is too absurd for common sense to admit any discussion upon. You know it is the blood of Jesus Christ; it is the merit of his agonies; it is the purchase of his sufferings; it is what he did, that alone can save us. Venture on him; venture wholly, and then you are saved. Hearest thou, poor convinced sinner, the way of salvation? If I ever meet thee in the next world, thou mightest, perhaps, say to me, "I spent one evening, sir, in hearing you, and you never told me the way to heaven." Well, thou shalt hear it. Believe on the Lord Jesus Christ, trust in his righteousness, and thou art saved beyond the vengeance of the law, or the power of hell. But trust in thine own works, and thou art lost as sure as thou art alive.

Now, O ever glorious Son of God, we approach thy table to feast on the viands of grace, permit each of us, in reliance upon thy Spirit, to exclaim in the words of one of thine own poets:

"Remember thee, and all thy pains,
And all thy love to me—
Yes, while a pulse or breath remains,
I will remember thee.
And when these failing lips grow dumb,
And thought and memory flee;
When thou shalt in thy kingdom come,
Jesus, remember me!"

THE SIN OF UNBELIEF

A SERMON
(No. 3)

Delivered on Sabbath Evening, January 7th, 1855,
by the REV. C. H. Spurgeon
At New Park Street Chapel, Southwark,

"And that lord answered the man of God, and said,
Now, behold, if the Lord should make windows in
heaven, might such a thing be? And he said, Behold,
thou shalt see it with thine eyes but shalt not eat
thereof"—2 Kings 7:19.

ONE WISE man may deliver a whole city; one good
man may be the means of safety to a thousand others.
The holy ones are "the salt of the earth," the means of
the preservation of the wicked. Without the godly as a
conserve, the race would be utterly destroyed. In the
city of Samaria there was one righteous man—Elisha,
the servant of the Lord. Piety was altogether extinct in
the court. The king was a sinner of the blackest dye,
his iniquity was glaring and infamous. Jehoram walked
in the ways of his father Ahab, and made unto himself
false gods. The people of Samaria were fallen like their
monarch: they had gone astray from Jehovah; they had

forsaken the God of Israel; they remembered not the watchword of Jacob, "The Lord thy God is one God;" and in wicked idolatry they bowed before the idols of the heathens, and therefore the Lord of Hosts suffered their enemies to oppress them until the curse of Ebal was fulfilled in the streets of Samaria, for "the tender and delicate woman who would not adventure to set the sole of her foot upon the ground for delicateness," had an evil eye to her own children, and devoured her offspring by reason of fierce hunger (Deut 28:56–58). In this awful extremity the one holy man was the medium of salvation. The one grain of salt preserved the entire city; the one warrior for God was the means of the deliverance of the whole beleaguered multitude. For Elisha's sake the Lord sent the promise that the next day, food which could not be obtained at any price, should be had at the cheapest possible rate—at the very gates of Samaria. We may picture the joy of the multitude when first the seer uttered this prediction. They knew him to be a prophet of the Lord; he had divine credentials; all his past prophecies had been fulfilled. They knew that he was a man sent of God, and uttering Jehovah's message. Surely the monarch's eyes would glisten with delight, and the emaciated multitude would leap for joy at the prospects of so speedy a release from famine. "To-morrow," would they shout, "*to-morrow* our hunger shall be over, and we shall feast to the full."

However, the lord on whom the king leaned expressed his disbelief. We hear not that any of the common people, the plebeians, ever did so; but an aristocrat did it. Strange it is, that God has seldom chosen the great men of this world. High places and faith in Christ do seldom well agree. This great man said, "Impossible!" and, with an insult to the prophet, he added, "If the Lord should make windows in heaven, might such a thing be." His sin lay in the fact, that after repeated seals of Elisha's ministry, he yet disbelieved the assurances uttered by the prophet on God's behalf. He had, doubtless, seen the marvelous defeat of Moab; he had been startled at tidings of the resurrection of the Shunamite's son; he knew that Elisha had revealed Benhadad's secrets and smitten his marauding hosts with blindness; he had seen the bands of Syria decoyed into the heart of Samaria; and he probably knew the story of the widow, whose oil filled all the vessels, and redeemed her sons; at all events the cure of Naaman was common conversation at court; and yet, in the face of all this accumulated evidence, in the teeth of all these credentials of the prophet's mission, he yet doubted, and insultingly told him that heaven must become an open casement, ere the promise could be performed. Whereupon God pronounced his doom by the mouth of the man who had just now proclaimed the promise: "thou shalt see it with thine eyes, but shalt not eat thereof." And providence—which always fulfills prophecy, just as the paper takes the stamp of the type—destroyed the man. Trodden down in the streets of Samaria, he perished at its gates, beholding the plenty, but tasting not of it. Perhaps his carriage was haughty, and insulting to the people; or he tried to restrain their eager rush; or, as we would say, it might have been by mere accident that he was crushed to death; so that he saw the prophecy fulfilled, but never lived to enjoy it. In his case, seeing was believing, but it was not enjoying.

I shall this morning invite your attention to two things—the man's *sin* and his punishment. Perhaps I shall say but little of this man, since I have detailed the circumstances, but I shall discourse upon the sin of unbelief and the punishment thereof.

I. And first, the SIN.

His sin was *unbelief.* He doubted the promise of God. In this particular case unbelief took the form of a doubt of the divine veracity, or a mistrust of God's power. Either he doubted whether God really meant what he said, or whether it was within the range of possibility that God should fulfill his promise. Unbelief hath more phases than the moon, and more colors than the chameleon. Common people say of the devil, that he is seen sometimes in one shape, and sometimes in another. I am sure this is true of Satan's first-born child—unbelief, for its forms are legion. At one time I see unbelief dressed out as an angel of light. It calls itself humility, and it saith, "I would not be presumptuous; I dare not think that God would pardon me; I am too great a sinner." We call that humility, and thank God that our friend is in so good a condition. I do not thank God for any such delusion. It is the devil dressed as an angel of light; it is unbelief after all. At other times we detect unbelief in the shape of a doubt of God's immutability: "The Lord has loved me, but perhaps he will cast me off to-morrow. He helped me yesterday, and under the shadows of his wings I trust; but perhaps I shall receive no help in the next affliction. He may have cast me off; he may be unmindful of his covenant, and forget to be gracious." Sometimes this infidelity is embodied in a doubt of God's power. We see every day new straits, we are involved in a net of difficulties, and we think "surely the Lord cannot deliver us." We strive to get rid of our burden, and finding that we cannot do it, we think God's arm is as short as ours, and his power as little as human might. A fearful form of unbelief is that doubt which keeps men from coming to Christ; which leads the sinner to distrust the ability of Christ to save him, to doubt the willingness of Jesus to accept so great a transgressor. But the most hideous of all is the traitor, in its true colors, blaspheming God, and madly denying his existence. Infidelity, deism, and atheism, are the ripe fruits of this pernicious tree; they are the most terrific eruptions of the volcano of unbelief. Unbelief hath become of full stature, when quitting the mask and laying aside disguise, it profanely stalks the earth, uttering the rebellious cry, "No God," striving in vain to shake the throne of the divinity, by lifting up its arm against Jehovah, and in its arrogance would

> "Snatch from his hand the balance and the rod,
> Re-judge his justice—be the god of God."

Then truly unbelief has come to its full perfection, and then you see what it really is, for the least unbelief is of the same nature as the greatest.

I am astonished, and I am sure you will be, when I tell you that there are some strange people in the world who do not believe that unbelief is a sin. Strange people I must call them, because they are sound in their faith in every other respect; only, to make the articles of their creed consistent, as they imagine, they deny that unbelief is sinful. I remember a young man going into a circle of friends and ministers, who were disputing whether it was a sin in men that they did not believe the gospel. Whilst they were discussing it, he said, "Gentlemen am I in the presence of Christians? Are you believers in the Bible, or are you not?" They said, "We are Christians of course." "Then," said he, "does not the Scripture say, 'of sin, because they believed not on me?' And is it not the damning sin of sinners, that they do not believe on Christ?" I could not have thought that persons should be so fool-hardy as to venture to assert that, "it is no sin for a sinner not to believe on Christ." I thought that, however far they might wish to push their sentiments, they would not tell a lie to uphold the truth, and, in my opinion this is what such men are really doing. Truth is a strong tower and never requires to be buttressed with error. God's Word will stand against all man's devices. I would never invent a sophism to prove that it is no sin on the part of the ungodly not to believe, for I am sure it is, when I am taught in the Scriptures that, "This is the condemnation, that light is come into the world, and men love darkness rather than light," and when I read, "He that believeth not is condemned already, because he believeth not on the Son of God," I affirm, and the Word declares it, _unbelief is a sin_. Surely with rational and unprejudiced persons, it cannot require any reasoning to prove it. Is it not a sin for a creature to doubt the word of its Maker? Is it not a crime and an insult to the Divinity, for me, an atom, a particle of dust, to dare to deny his words? Is it not the very summit of arrogance and extremity of pride for a son of Adam to say, even in his heart, "God I doubt thy grace; God I doubt thy love; God I doubt thy power?" Oh! sirs believe me, could ye roll all sins into one mass,—could you take murder, and blasphemy, and lust, adultery, and fornication, and everything that is vile and unite them all into one vast globe of black corruption, they would not equal even then the sin of unbelief. This is the monarch sin, the quintessence of guilt; the mixture of the venom of all crimes; the dregs of the wine of Gomorrah; it is the A1 sin, the master-piece of Satan, the chief work of the devil.

I shall attempt this morning, for a little while, to shew the extremely evil nature of the sin of unbelief.

1. And first the sin of unbelief will appear to be extremely heinous when we remember that *it is the parent of every other iniquity*. There is no crime which unbelief will not beget. I think that the fall of man is very much owing to it. It was in this point that the devil tempted Eve. He said to her, "Yea, *hath* God said, ye shall not eat of every tree of the garden?" He whispered and insinuated a doubt, "Yea, *hath* God said so?" as much as to say, "Are you *quite* sure he said so?" It was by means of unbelief—that thin part of the wedge—that the other sin entered; curiosity and the rest followed; she touched the fruit, and destruction came into this world. Since that time, unbelief has been the prolific parent of all guilt. An unbeliever is capable of the vilest crime that ever was committed. Unbelief, sirs! why it hardened the heart of Pharaoh—it gave license to the tongue of blaspheming Rabshaket—yea, it became a deicide, and murdered Jesus. Unbelief!—it has sharpened the

knife of the suicide! it has mixed many a cup of poison; thousands it has brought to the halter; and many to a shameful grave, who have murdered themselves and rushed with bloody hands before their Creator's tribunal, because of unbelief. Give me an unbeliever—let me know that he doubts God's word—let me know that he distrusts his promise and his threatening; and with that for a premise, I will conclude that the man shall, by-and-bye unless there is amazing restraining power exerted upon him, be guilty of the foulest and blackest crimes. Ah! this is a Beelzebub sin; like Beelzebub, it is the leader of all evil spirits. It is said of Jeroboam that he sinned and made Israel to sin; and it may be said of unbelief that it not only sins itself, but makes others sin; it is the egg of all crime, the seed of every offence; in fact everything that is evil and vile lies couched in that one word—unbelief.

And let me say here, that unbelief in the Christian is of the self-same nature as unbelief in the sinner. It is not the same in its final issue, for it will be pardoned in the Christian; yea it is pardoned: it was laid upon the scapegoat's head of old: it was blotted out and atoned for; but it is of the same sinful nature. In fact, if there can be one sin more heinous than the unbelief of a sinner, it is the unbelief of a saint. For a saint to doubt God's word—for a saint to distrust God after innumerable instances of his love, after ten thousand proofs of his mercy, exceeds everything. In a saint, moreover, unbelief is the root of other sins. When I am perfect in faith, I shall be perfect in everything else; I should always fulfill the precept if I always believed the promise. But it is because my faith is weak, that I sin. Put me in trouble, and if I can fold my arms and say, "Jehovah-Jireh, the Lord will provide," you will not find me using wrong means to escape from it. But let me be in temporal distress and difficulty; if I distrust God, what then? Perhaps I shall steal, or do a dishonest act to get out of the hands of my creditors; or if kept from such a transgression, I may plunge into excess to drown my anxieties. Once take away faith, the reins are broken; and who can ride an unbroken steed without rein or bridle? Like the chariot of the sun, with Phaeton for its driver, such should we be without faith. Unbelief is the mother of vice; it is the parent of sin; and, therefore, I say it is a pestilent evil—a master sin.

2. But secondly; *unbelief not only begets, but fosters sin.* How is it that men can keep their sin under the thunders of the Sinai preacher? How is it that, when Boanerges stands in the pulpit, and, by the grace of God, cries aloud, "Cursed is every man that keepeth not all the commands of the law,"—how is it that when the sinner hears the tremendous threatenings of God's justice, still he is hardened, and walks on in his evil ways? I will tell you; it is because unbelief of that threatening prevents it from having any effect upon him. When our sappers

and miners go to work around Sebastopol, they could not work in front of the walls, if they had not something to keep off the shots; so they raise earthworks, behind which they can do what they please. So with the ungodly man. The devil gives him unbelief; he thus puts up an earthwork, and finds refuge behind it. Ah! sinners, when once the Holy Ghost knocks down your unbelief—when once he brings home the truth in demonstration and in power, how the law will work upon your soul. If man did but believe that the law is holy, that the commandments are holy, just, and good, how he would be shaken over hell's mouth; there would be no sitting and sleeping in God's house; no careless hearers; no going away and straightway forgetting what manner of men ye are. Oh! once get rid of unbelief, how would ever ball from the batteries of the law fall upon the sinner, and the slain of the Lord would be many. Again, how is it that men can hear the wooing of the cross of Calvary, and yet come not to Christ? How is it that when we preach about the sufferings of Jesus, and close up by saying, "yet there is room,"—how is it that when we dwell upon his cross and passion, men are not broken in their hearts? It is said,

> "Law and terrors do but harden,
> All the while they work alone:
> But a sense of blood-bought pardon
> Will dissolve a heart of stone."

Methinks the tale of Calvary is enough to break a rock. Rocks did rend when they saw Jesus die. Methinks the tragedy of Golgotha is enough to make a flint gush with tears, and to make the most hardened wretch weep out his eyes in drops of penitential love; but yet we tell it you, and repeat it oft, but who weeps over it? Who cares about it? Sirs, ye sit as unconcerned as if it did not signify to you. Oh! behold and see all ye that pass by. Is it nothing to you that Jesus should die? Ye seem to say "It is nothing." What is the reason? Because there is unbelief between you and the cross. If there were not that thick veil between you and the Saviour's eyes, his looks of love would melt you. But unbelief is the sin which keeps the power of the gospel from working in the sinner: and it is not till the Holy Ghost strikes that unbelief out—it is not till the Holy Spirit rends away that infidelity and takes it altogether down, that we can find the sinner coming to put his trust in Jesus.

3. But there is a third point. *Unbelief disables a man for the performance of any good work.* "Whatsoever is not of faith is sin," is a great truth in more senses than one. "Without faith it is impossible to please God." You shall never hear me say a word against morality; you shall never hear me say that honesty is not a good thing, or that sobriety is not a good thing; on the contrary, I would say they are commendable things; but I will tell you what I will say afterwards—I will tell you that they are just like the

cowries of Hindostan; they may pass current among the Indians, but they will not do in England; these virtues may be current here below, but not above. If you have not something better than your own goodness, you will never get to heaven. Some of the Indian tribes use little strips of cloth instead of money, and I would not find fault with them if I lived there; but when I come to England, strips of cloth will not suffice. So honesty, sobriety, and such things, may be very good amongst men—and the more you have of them the better. I exhort you, whatsoever things are lovely and pure, and of good report, have them—but they will not do up there. All these things put together, without faith, do not please God. Virtues without faith are whitewashed sins. Obedience without faith, if it is possible, is a gilded disobedience. Not to believe, nullifies everything. It is the fly in the ointment; it is the poison in the pot. Without faith, with all the virtues of purity, with all the benevolence of philanthropy, with all the kindness of disinterested sympathy, with all the talents of genius, with all the bravery of patriotism, and with all the decision of principle—"without faith it is impossible to please God." Do you not see then, how bad unbelief is, because it prevents men from performing good works. Yea, even in Christians themselves, unbelief disables them. Let me just tell you a tale—a story of Christ's life. A certain man had an afflicted son, possessed with an evil spirit. Jesus was up in Mount Tabor, transfigured;

so the father brought his son to the disciples. What did the disciples do? They said, "Oh, we will cast him out." They put their hands upon him, and they tried to do it; but they whispered among themselves and said, "We are afraid we shall not be able." By-and-by the diseased man began to froth at the mouth; he foamed and scratched the earth, clasping it in his paroxysms. The demoniac spirit within him was alive. The devil was still there. In vain their repeated exorcism, the evil spirit remained like a lion in his den, nor could their efforts dislodge him. "Go!" said they; but he went not. "Away to the pit!" they cried; but he remained immoveable. The lips of unbelief cannot affright the Evil One, who might well have said, "Faith I know, Jesus I know, but who are ye? ye have no faith." If they had faith, as a grain of mustard seed, they might have cast the devil out; but their faith was gone, and therefore they could do nothing. Look at poor Peter's case, too. While he had faith, Peter walked on the waves of the sea. That was a splendid walk; I almost envy him treading upon the billows. Why, if Peter's faith had continued, he might have walked across the Atlantic to America. But presently there came a billow behind him, and he said, "That will sweep me away;" and then another before, and he cried out, "That will overwhelm me;" and he thought—how could I be so presumptuous as to be walking on the top of these waves? Down goes Peter. Faith was Peter's life-buoy; faith was Peter's charm—it kept him up; but unbelief sent him down. Do you know that you and I, all our lifetime, will have to walk on the water? A Christian's life is always walking on water—mine is—and every wave would swallow and devour him, but faith makes him stand. The moment you cease to believe, that moment distress comes in, and down you go. Oh! wherefore dost thou doubt, then?

Faith fosters every virtue; unbelief murders every one. Thousands of prayers have been strangled in their infancy by unbelief. Unbelief has been guilty of infanticide; it has murdered many an infant petition; many a song of praise that would have swelled the chorus of the skies, has been stifled by an unbelieving murmur; many a noble enterprise conceived in the heart has been blighted ere it could come forth, by unbelief. Many a man would have been a missionary; would have stood and preached his Master's gospel boldly; but he had unbelief. Once make a giant unbelieving, and he becomes a dwarf. Faith is the Samsonian lock of the Christian; cut it off, and you may put out his eyes—and he can do nothing.

4. Our next remark is—*unbelief has been severely punished*. Turn you to the Scriptures! I see a world all fair and beautiful; its mountains laughing in the sun, and the fields rejoicing in the golden light. I see maidens dancing, and young men singing. How fair the vision! But lo! a grave and reverend sire lifts up his hand, and cries, "A flood

is coming to deluge the earth: the fountains of the great deep will be broken up, and all things will be covered. See yonder ark! One hundred and twenty years have I toiled with these my hands to build it; flee there, and you are safe." "Aha! old man; away with your empty predictions! Aha! let us be happy while we may! when the flood comes, then we will build an ark; but there is no flood coming; tell that to fools; we believe no such things." See the unbelievers pursue their merry dance. Hark! Unbeliever. Dost thou not hear that rumbling noise? Earth's bowels have begun to move, her rocky ribs are strained by dire convulsions from within; lo! they break with the enormous strain, and forth from between them torrents rush unknown since God concealed them in the bosom of our world. Heaven is split in sunder! it rains. Not drops, but clouds descend. A cataract, like that of old Niagara, rolls from heaven with mighty noise. Both firmaments, both deeps—the deep below and deep above—do clasp their hands. Now unbelievers, where are you now! There is your last remnant. A man—his wife clasping him round the waist—stands on the last summit that is above the water. See him there? The water is up to his loins even now. Hear his last shriek! He is floating—he is drowned. And as Noah looks from the ark he sees nothing. Nothing! It is a void profound. "Sea monsters whelp and stable in the palaces of kings." All is overthrown, covered, drowned. What hath done it? What brought the flood upon the earth? Unbelief. By faith Noah escaped from the flood. By unbelief the rest were drowned.

And, oh! do you not know that unbelief kept Moses and Aaron out of Canaan? They honored not God; they struck the rock when they ought to have spoken to it. They disbelieved: and therefore the punishment came upon them, that they should not inherit that good land, for which they had toiled and labored.

Let me take you where Moses and Aaron dwelt—to the vast and howling wilderness. We will walk about it for a time; sons of the weary foot, we will become like the wandering Bedouins, we will tread the desert for a while. There lies a carcass whitened in the sun; there another, and there another. What means these bleached bones? What are these bodies—there a man, and there a woman? What are all these? How came these corpses here? Surely some grand encampment must have been here cut off in a single night by a blast, or by bloodshed. Ah; no, no. Those bones are the bones of Israel; those skeletons are the old tribes of Jacob. They could not enter because of unbelief. They trusted not in God. Spies said they could not conquer the land. Unbelief was the cause of their death. It was not the Anakims that destroyed Israel; it was not the howling wilderness which devoured them; it was not the Jordan which proved a barrier to Canaan; neither Hivite or Jebusite slew them; it was unbelief alone which kept them out of Canaan. What a doom to be pronounced on Israel, after forty years of journeying: they could not enter because of unbelief!

Not to multiply instances, recollect Zechariah. He doubted, and the angel struck him dumb. His mouth was closed because of unbelief. But oh! if you would have the worst picture of the effects of unbelief—if you would see how God has punished it, I must take you to the siege of Jerusalem, that worst massacre which time has ever seen; when the Romans razed the walls to the ground, and put the whole of the inhabitants to the sword, or sold them as slaves in the market-place. Have you never read of the destruction of Jerusalem, by Titus? Did you never turn to the tragedy of Masada, when the Jews stabbed each other rather than fall into the hands of the Romans? Do you not know, that to this day the Jew walks through the earth a wanderer, without a home and without a land? He is cut off, as a branch is cut from a vine; and why? Because of unbelief. Each time ye see a Jew with a sad and somber countenance—each time ye mark him like a denizen of another land, treading as an exile in this our country—each time ye see him, pause and say, "Ah! it was unbelief which caused thee to murder Christ, and now it has driven thee to be a wanderer; and faith alone—faith in the crucified Nazarene—can fetch thee back to thy country, and restore it to its ancient grandeur." Unbelief, you see, has the Cain-mark upon its forehead. God hates it; God has dealt hard blows upon it: and God will ultimately crush it. Unbelief dishonors God. Every other crime touches God's territory; but unbelief aims a blow at his divinity, impeaches his veracity, denies his goodness, blasphemes his attributes, maligns his character; therefore, God of all things, hates first and chiefly, unbelief, wherever it is.

5. And now to close this point—for I have been already too long—let me remark that you will observe the heinous nature of unbelief in this—that it is the damning sin. There is one sin for which Christ never died; *it is the sin* against the Holy Ghost. There is one other sin for which Christ never made atonement. Mention every crime in the calendar of evil, and I will show you persons who have found forgiveness for it. But ask me whether the man who died in unbelief can be saved, and I reply there is no atonement for that man. There is an atonement made for the unbelief of a Christian, because it is temporary; but the final unbelief—the unbelief with which men die—never was atoned for. You may turn over this whole Book, and you will find that there is no atonement for the man who died in unbelief; there is no mercy for him. Had he been guilty of every other sin, if he had but believed, he would have been pardoned; but this is the damning exception—he had no faith. Devils seize him! O fiends of the pit, drag him downward to

his doom! He is faithless and unbelieving, and such are the tenants for whom hell was built. It is *their* portion, *their* prison, they are the chief prisoners, the fetters are marked with their names, and for ever shall they know that, "he that believeth not shall be damned."

II. This brings us now to conclude with the PUNISHMENT.

"Thou shalt see it with thine eyes, but shalt not eat thereof." Listen unbelievers! ye have heard this morning your sin; now listen to your doom: "Ye shall see it with your eyes, but shalt not eat thereof." It is so often with God's own saints. When they are unbelieving, they see the mercy with their eyes, but do not eat it. Now, here is corn in this land of Egypt; but there are some of God's saints who come here on the Sabbath, and say, "I do not know whether the Lord will be with me or not." Some of them say, "Well, the gospel is preached, but I do not know whether it will be successful." They are always doubting and fearing. Listen to them when they get out of the chapel. "Well, did you get a good meal this morning?" "Nothing for me." Of course not. Ye could see it with your eyes, but did not eat it, because you had no faith. If you had come up with faith, you would have had a morsel. I have found Christians, who have grown so very critical, that if the whole portion of the meat they are to have, in due season, is not cut up exactly into square pieces, and put upon some choice dish of porcelain, they cannot eat it. Then they ought to go without; and they will have to go without, until they are brought to their appetites. They will have some affliction, which will act like quinine upon them: they will be made to eat by means of bitters in their mouths; they will be put in prison for a day or two until their appetite returns, and then they will be glad to eat the most ordinary food, off the most common platter, or no platter at all. But the real reason why God's people do not feed under a gospel ministry, is, because they have not faith. If you believed, if you did but hear one promise, that would be enough; if you only heard one good thing from the pulpit here would be food for your soul, for it is not the quantity we hear, but the quantity we believe, that does us good—it is that which we receive into our hearts with true and lively faith, that is our profit.

But, let me apply this chiefly to the unconverted. They often see great works of God done with their eyes, but they do not eat thereof. A crowd of people have come here this morning to see with their eyes, but I doubt whether all of them eat. Men cannot eat with their eyes, for if they could, most would be well fed. And, spiritually, persons cannot feed simply with their ears, nor simply with looking at the preacher; and so we find the majority of our congregations come just to see; "Ah, let us hear what this babbler would say, this reed shaken in the wind." But they have no faith; they come, and they see, and see, and see, and never eat. There is some one in the front there, who gets converted; and some one down below, who is called by sovereign grace; some poor sinner is weeping under a sense of his blood-guiltiness; another is crying for mercy to God: and another is saying, "Have mercy upon me, a sinner." A great work is going on in this chapel, but some of you do not know anything about it; you have no work going on in your hearts, and why? Because ye think it is impossible; ye think God is not at work. He has not promised to work for you who do not honor him. Unbelief makes you sit here in times of revival and of the outpouring of God's grace, unmoved, uncalled, unsaved.

But, sirs, the worst fulfillment of this doom is to come! Good Whitefield used sometimes to lift up both his hands and shout, as I wish I could shout, but my voice fails me. "The wrath to come! the wrath to come!" It is not the wrath now you have to fear, but the wrath to come; and there shall be a doom to come, when "ye shall see it with your eyes, but shall not eat thereof." Methinks I see the last great day. The last hour of time has struck. I heard the bell toll its death knell—time was, eternity is ushered in; the sea is boiling; the waves are lit up with supernatural splendour. I see a rainbow—a flying cloud, and on it there is a throne, and on that throne sits one like unto the Son of Man. I know him. In his hand he holds a pair of balances; just before him the books,—the book of life, the book of death, the book of remembrance. I see his splendour, and I rejoice at it; I behold his pompous appearance, and I smile with gladness that he is come to be "admired of all his saints." But there stands a throng of miserable wretches, crouching in horror to conceal themselves, and yet looking, for their eyes must look on him whom they have pierced; but when they look they cry, "Hide me from the face." What face? "Rocks, hide me from the face." What face? "The face of Jesus, the man who died, but now is come to judgment." But ye cannot be hidden from his face; ye must see it with your eyes: but ye will not sit on the right hand, dressed in robes of grandeur; and when the triumphal procession of Jesus in the clouds shall come, ye shall not march in it; ye shall see it, but ye shall not be there. Oh! methinks I see it now, the mighty Saviour in his chariot, riding on the rainbow to heaven. See how his mighty coursers make the sky rattle while he drives them up heaven's hill. A train girt in white follow behind him, and at his chariot wheels he drags the devil, death, and hell. Hark, how they clap their hands. Hark, how they shout. "Thou hast ascended up on high; thou hast led captivity captive." Hark, how they chant the solemn lay, "Hallelujah, the Lord God omnipotent reigneth." See the splendour of their appearance; mark the crown upon their brows; see their snow-white garments; mark the rapture of their countenances; hear how their song swells up to heaven while the Eternal joins therein, saying, "I will rejoice over them with joy, I will rejoice over them with singing, for I have betrothed thee unto me in everlasting lovingkindness." But where are you all the while? Ye can see them up there, but where are you? Looking at it with your eyes, but you cannot eat thereof. The marriage banquet is spread; the good old wines of eternity are broached; they sit down to the feast of the king; but there are you, miserable, and famishing, and ye cannot eat thereof. Oh! how ye wring your hands. Might ye but have one morsel from the table—might ye but be dogs beneath the table. You shall be a dog in hell, but not a dog in heaven.

But to conclude. Methinks I see thee in some place in hell, tied to a rock, the vulture of remorse gnawing thy heart; and up there is Lazarus in Abraham's bosom. You lift up your eyes and you see who it is. "That is the poor man who lay on my dunghill, and the dogs licked his sores; there he is in heaven, while I am cast down. Lazarus—yes, it is Lazarus; and I who was rich in the world of time am here in hell. Father Abraham, send Lazarus, that he may dip the tip of his finger in water, to cool my tongue." But no! it cannot be; it cannot be. And whilst you lie there, if there be one thing in hell worse than another, it will be seeing the saints in heaven. Oh, to think of seeing my mother in heaven while I am cast out! Oh, sinner, only think, to see thy brother in heaven—he who was rocked in the selfsame cradle, and played beneath the same roof-tree—yet thou art cast out. And, husband, there is thy wife in heaven, and thou art amongst the damned. And seest thou, father! thy child is before the throne; and thou! accursed of God and accursed of man, art in hell. Oh, the hell of hells will be to see our friends in heaven, and ourselves lost. I beseech you, my hearers, by the death of Christ—by his agony and bloody sweat—by his cross and passion—by all that is holy—by all that is sacred in heaven and earth—by all that is solemn in time or eternity—by all that is horrible in hell, or glorious in heaven —by that awful thought, "for ever,"—I beseech you lay these things to heart, and remember that if you are damned, it will be unbelief that damns you. If you are lost, it will be because ye believed not on Christ; and if you perish, this shall be the bitterest drop of gall—that ye did not trust in the Saviour.

PERSONALITY OF THE HOLY GHOST

A SERMON
(No. 4)

Delivered on Sabbath Morning, January 21th, 1855,
by the REV. C. H. Spurgeon
At New Park Street Chapel, Southwark,

"And I will pray the Father, and he shall give you
another Comforter, that he may abide with you for
ever; even the Spirit of truth; whom the world cannot
receive, because it seeth him not, neither knoweth
him: but ye know him; for he dwelleth with you,
and shall be in you."—John 14:16-17

YOU WILL be surprised to hear me announce that I do
not intend this morning to say anything about the Holy
Spirit as the Comforter. I propose to reserve that for
a special Sermon this evening. In this discourse I shall
endeavor to explain and enforce certain other doctrines,
which I believe are plainly taught in this text, and which
I hope God the Holy Ghost may make profitable to
our souls. Old John Newton once said, that there were
some books which he could not read;—they were
good and sound enough; but, said he, "they are books

of halfpence;—you have to take so much in quantity before you have any value; there are other books of silver, and others of gold; but I have one book that is a book of bank notes; and every leaf is a bank-note of immense value." So I found with this text: that I had a bank-note of so large a sum, that I could not tell it out all this morning. I should have to keep you several hours before I could unfold to you the whole value of this precious promise—one of the last which Christ gave his people.

I invite your attention to this passage because we shall find in it some instruction on four points: first, concerning the true and proper personality of the Holy Ghost; secondly, concerning the united agency of the glorious Three Persons in the work of our salvation; thirdly we shall find something to establish the doctrine of the indwelling of the Holy Ghost in the souls of all believers; and fourthly, we shall find out the reason why the carnal mind rejects the Holy Ghost.

I. First of all, we shall have some little instruction concerning the proper *personality of the Holy Spirit.* We are so much accustomed to talk about the influence of the Holy Ghost and his sacred operations and graces, that we are apt to forget that the Holy Spirit is truly and actually a person—that he is a subsistence—an existence; or, as we Trinitarians usually say, one person in the essence of the Godhead. I am afraid that, though we do not know it, we have acquired the habit of regarding the Holy Ghost as an emanation flowing from the Father and the Son, but not as being actually a person himself. I know it is not easy to carry about in our mind the idea of the Holy Spirit as a person. I can think of the Father as a person, because his acts are such as I can understand. I see him hang the world in ether; I behold him swaddling a new-born sea in bands of darkness; I know it is he who formed the drops of hail, who leadeth forth the stars by their hosts, and calleth them by their name; I can conceive of Him as a person, because I behold his operations. I can realize Jesus, the Son of Man, as a real person, because he is bone of my bone and flesh of my flesh. It takes no great stretch of my imagination to picture the babe in Bethlehem, or to behold the "Man of sorrows and acquainted with grief," of the king of martyrs, as he was persecuted in Pilate's hall, or nailed to the accursed tree for our sins. Nor do I find it difficult at times to realize the person of my Jesus sitting on his throne in heaven; or girt with clouds and wearing the diadem of all creation, calling the earth to judgment, and summoning us to hear our final sentence. But when I come to deal with the Holy Ghost, his operations are so mysterious, his doings are so secret, his acts are so removed from everything that is of sense, and of the body, that I cannot so easily get the idea of his being a person; but a person he is. God the

Holy Ghost is not an influence, an emanation, a stream of something flowing from the Father; but he is as much an actual person as either God the Son, or God the Father. I shall attempt this morning a little to establish the doctrine, and to show you the truth of it—that God the Holy Spirit is actually a person.

The first proof we shall gather from the pool of holy baptism. Let me take you down, as I have taken others, into the pool, now concealed, but which I wish were always open to your view. Let me take you to the baptismal font, where believers put on the name of the Lord Jesus, and you shall hear me pronounce the solemn words, "I baptize thee in the name,"—mark, "in the name," not names—"of the Father, and of the Son, and of the Holy Ghost." Every one who is baptized according to the true form laid down in Scripture, must be a Trinitarian: otherwise his baptism is a farce and a lie, and he himself is found a deceiver and a hypocrite before God. As the Father is mentioned, and as the Son is mentioned, so is the Holy Ghost; and the whole is summed up as being a Trinity in unity, by its being said, not the names, but the "name" the glorious name, the Jehovah name, "of the Father, and of the Son, and of the Holy Ghost." Let me remind you that the same thing occurs each time you are dismissed from this house of prayer. In pronouncing the solemn closing benediction, we invoke on your behalf the love of Jesus Christ, the grace of the Father, and the fellowship of the Holy Spirit; and thus, according to the apostolic manner, we make a manifest distinction between the persons, showing that we believe the Father to be a person, the Son to be a person, and the Holy Ghost to be a person. Were there no other proofs in Scripture, I think these would be sufficient for every sensible man. He would see that if the Holy Spirit were a mere influence, he would not be mentioned in conjunction with two whom we all confess to be actual and proper persons.

A second argument arises from the fact that the Holy Ghost has actually made different appearances on earth. The Great Spirit has manifested himself to man: he has put on a form, so that, whilst he has not been beheld by mortal men, he has been so veiled in appearance that he was seen, so far as that appearance was concerned, by the eyes of all beholders. See you Jesus Christ our Saviour? There is the river Jordan, with its shelving banks and its willows weeping at its side. Jesus Christ, the Son of God, descends into the stream, and the holy Baptist, John, plunges him into the waves. The doors of heaven are opened; a miraculous appearance presents itself; a bright light shineth from the sky, brighter than the sun in all its grandeur, and down in a flood of glory descends something which you recognize to be a dove. It rests on Jesus—it sits upon his sacred head, and as the old painters put a halo round the brow of Jesus, so did the Holy Ghost shed a resplendence around the face of him who came to fulfil all righteousness, and therefore commenced with the ordinance of baptism. The Holy Ghost was seen as a dove, to mark his purity and his gentleness, and he came down like a dove *from heaven* to show that it is from heaven alone that he descendeth. Nor is this the only time when the Holy Ghost has been manifest in a visible shape. You see that company of disciples gathered together in an upper room; they are waiting for some promised blessing, and bye-and-bye it shall come. Hark! there is a sound as of a rushing mighty wind; it fills all the house where they are sitting; and astonished, they look around them, wondering what will come next. Soon a bright light appears, shining upon the heads of each: cloven tongues of fire sat upon them. What were these marvelous appearances of wind and flame but a display of the Holy Ghost in his proper person? I say the fact of an appearance manifests that he must be a person. An influence could not appear—an attribute could not appear: we cannot see attributes—we cannot behold influences. The Holy Ghost must, then, have been a person; since he was beheld by mortal eyes, and he came under the cognizance of mortal sense.

Another proof is from the fact, that personal qualities are, in Scripture, ascribed to the Holy Ghost. First, let me read to you a text in which the Holy Ghost is spoken of as having *understanding*. In the 1st Epistle to the Corinthians, chap. ii., you will read, "But as it is written, eye hath not seen, nor ear heard, neither hath it entered into the heart of man, the things which God hath prepare for them that love him. But God have revealed them unto us by his Spirit: for the Spirit searcheth all things, yea, the deep things of God. For what man knoweth the things of a man, save the spirit of man which is in him? Even so the things of God knoweth no man, but the Spirit of God." Here you see an understanding—a power of knowledge is ascribed to the Holy Ghost. Now, if there be any persons here whose minds are of so preposterous a complexion that they would ascribe one attribute to another, and would speak of a mere influence having understanding, then I give up all the argument. But I believe every rational man will admit, that when anything is spoken of as having an understanding, it must be an existence—it must, in fact, be a person. In the 12th chap., 11th verse of the same Epistle, you will find a *will* ascribed to the Holy Spirit. "But all these worketh that one and the self-same spirit, dividing to every man severally as he will." So it is plain that the Spirit has a will. He does not come from God simply at God's will, but he has a will of his own, which is always in keeping with the will of the infinite Jehovah, but is, nevertheless, distinct and separate; therefore, I say he is a person. In another text, *power* is ascribed to the Holy Ghost, and power is a thing which can only be ascribed to an existence. In Romans

15:13, it is written, "Now the God of hope fill you with all joy and peace in believing, that ye may abound in hope through the power of the Holy Ghost." I need not insist upon it, because it is self-evident, that wherever you find understanding, will, and power, you must also find an existence; it cannot be a mere attribute, it cannot be a metaphor, it cannot be a personified influence; but it must be a person.

But I have a proof which, perhaps, will be more telling upon you than any other. Acts and deeds are ascribed to the Holy Ghost; therefore, he must be a person. You read in the first chapter of the Book of Genesis, that the Spirit brooded over the surface of the earth, when it was as yet all disorder and confusion. This world was once a mass of chaotic matter, there was no order; it was like the valley of darkness and of the shadow of death. God the Holy Ghost spread his wings over it; he sowed the seeds of life in it; the germs from which all beings sprang were implanted by him; he impregnated the earth so that it became capable of life. Now, it must have been a person who brought order out of confusion: it must have been an existence who hovered over this world and made it what it now is. But do we not read in Scripture something more of the Holy Ghost? Yes, we are told that "holy men of old spake as they were moved by the Holy Ghost." When Moses penned the Pentateuch, the Holy Ghost moved his hand; when

David wrote the Psalms, and discoursed sweet music on his harp, it was the Holy Spirit that gave his fingers their seraphic motion; when Solomon dropped from his lips the words of the proverbs of wisdom, or when he hymned the Canticles of love, it was the Holy Ghost who gave him words of knowledge and hymns of rapture. Ah! and what fire was that which touched the lips of the eloquent Isaiah? What hand was that which came upon Daniel? What might was that which made Jeremiah so plaintive in his grief? or what was that which winged Ezekiel and made him like an eagle, soar into mysteries aloft, and see the mighty unknown beyond our reach? Who was it that made Amos, the herdsman, a prophet? Who taught the rugged Haggai to pronounce his thundering sentences? Who showed Habakkuk the horses of Jehovah marching through the waters? or who kindled the burning eloquence of Nahum? Who caused Malachi to close up the book with the muttering of the word curse? Who was it in each of these, save the Holy Ghost? And must it not have been a person who spake in and through these ancient witnesses? We must believe it. We cannot avoid believing it, when we read that "holy men of old spake as they were moved by the Holy Ghost."

And when has the Holy Ghost ceased to have an influence upon men? We find that still he deals with his ministers and with all his saints. Turn to the Acts, and you will find that the Holy Ghost said, "Separate me Paul and Barnabas for the work." I never heard of an attribute saying such a thing. The Holy Spirit said to Peter, "Go to the Centurion, and what I have cleansed, that call not thou common." The Holy Ghost caught away Philip after he had baptized the Eunuch, and carried him away to another place; and the Holy Ghost said to Paul; "Thou shalt not go into that city, but shall turn into another." And we know that the Holy Ghost was lied unto by Ananias and Sapphira, when it was said, "Thou hast not lied unto man, but unto God." Again, that power which we feel every day, who are called to preach—that wondrous spell which makes our lips so potent—that power which gives us thoughts which are like birds from a far-off region, not the natives of our soul—that influence which I sometimes strangely feel, which, if it does not give me poetry and eloquence, gives me a might I never felt before, and lifts me above my fellow-man—that majesty with which he clothes his ministers, till in the midst of the battle they cry aha! like the war-horse of Job, and move themselves like leviathans in the water—that power which gives us might over men, and causes them to sit and listen as if their ears were chained, as if they were entranced by the power of some magician's wand—that power must come from a person; it must come from the Holy Ghost.

But is it not said in Scripture, and do we not feel it, dear brethren, that it is the Holy Ghost who regenerates the soul? It is the Holy Ghost who quickens us. "You hath he quickened who were dead in trespasses and sins." It is the Holy Spirit who imparts the first germ of life, convincing us of sin, of righteousness, and of judgment to come. And is it not the Holy Spirit, who, after that flame is kindled, still fans it with the breath of his mouth and keeps it alive? Its author is its preserver. Oh! can it be said that it is the Holy Ghost who strives in men's souls; that it is the Holy Ghost who brings them into the sweet place that is called Calvary—can it be said that he does all these things, and yet is not a person? It may be said, but it must be said by fools; for he never can be a wise man who can consider these things can be done by any other than a glorious person—a divine existence.

Allow me to give you one more proof, and I shall have done. Certain feelings are ascribed to the Holy Ghost, which can only be understood upon the supposition that he is actually a person. In the 4th chapter of Ephesians, v. 30, it is said that the Holy Ghost can be grieved: "Grieve not the Holy Spirit of God, whereby ye are sealed unto the day of redemption." In Isaiah, chap. lxiii, v. 10, it is said that the Holy Ghost can be vexed: "But they rebelled, and vexed his Holy Spirit; therefore he was turned to be their enemy., and he fought against them." In Acts, chap. vii. v. 51, you read that the Holy Ghost can be resisted: "Ye stiff-necked and uncircumcised in heart and ears, ye do always resist the Holy Ghost; as your fathers did, so do ye." And in the 5th chapter, v. 9, of the same book, you will find that the Holy Ghost may be tempted. We are informed that Peter said to Ananias and Sapphira, "How is it that ye have agreed together to tempt the Spirit of the Lord?" Now, these things could not be emotions which might be ascribed to a quality or an emanation; they must be understood to relate to a person; an influence could not be grieved, it must be a person who can be grieved, vexed, or resisted.

And now, dear brethren, I think I have fully established the point of the personality of the Holy Ghost; allow me now, most earnestly, to impress upon you the absolute necessity of being sound on the doctrine of the Trinity. I knew a man, a good minister of Jesus Christ he is now, and I believe he was before he turned his eyes unto heresy—he began to doubt the glorious divinity of our blessed Lord, and for years did he preach the heterodox doctrine, until one day he happened to hear a very eccentric old minister preaching from the text, "But there the *glorious Lord* shall be unto us a place of broad rivers and streams, wherein shall go no galley with oars, neither shall gallant ship pass thereby. Thy tacklings are loosed; they could not well strengthen their mast, they could not spread the sail." "Now," said the old minister, "you give up the Trinity, and your tacklings are loosed, you cannot strengthen your masts. Once give up the doctrine of three persons, and your tacklings are all gone; your mast, which ought to be a support to your vessel, is a rickety one, and shakes." A gospel without the Trinity! it is a pyramid built upon its apex. A gospel without the Trinity! it is a rope of sand that cannot hold together. A gospel without the Trinity! then, indeed, Satan can overturn it. But give me a gospel with the Trinity, and the might of hell cannot prevail against it; no man can any more overthrow it than a bubble could split a rock, or a feather break in halves a mountain. Get the thought of the three persons, and you have the marrow of all divinity. Only know the Father, and know the Son, and know the Holy Ghost to be one, and all things will appear clear. This is the golden key to the secrets of nature; this is the silken clue of the labyrinths of mystery, and he who understands this, will soon understand as much as mortals e'er can know.

II. Now for our second point—the *united agency* of the three persons in the work of our salvation. Look at the text, and you will find all the three persons mentioned. "I"—that is the Son—"will pray the Father, and he shall give you another Comforter." There are the three persons mentioned, all of them doing something for our salvation. "I will pray," says the Son. "I will send," says the Father. "I will comfort," says the Holy Ghost. now, let us, for a few moments, discourse upon this wondrous theme—the unity of the three persons with regard to the great purpose of the salvation of the elect. When God first made man, he said, "Let *us* make man," not let *me*, but, "Let us make man in our own image." The covenant Elohim said to each other, "Let us unitedly become the creator of man." So, when in ages far gone by, in eternity, they said, "Let us save man:" it was not the Father who said, "Let *me* save man, "but the three persons conjointly said, with one consent, "Let *us* save man." It is to me a source of sweet comfort to think that it is not one person of the Trinity that is engaged for my salvation; it is not simply one person of the Godhead who vows that he will redeem me; but it is a glorious trio of Godlike ones, and the three declare, unitedly, "*We* will save man."

Now, observe here, that each person is spoken of as performing a separate office. "I will pray," says the Son; that is intercession. "I will send," says the Father; that is donation. "I will comfort," says the Holy Spirit; that is supernatural influence. O! if it were possible for us to see the three persons of the Godhead, we should behold one of them standing before the throne, with outstretched hands, crying day and night, "O, Lord, how long?" We should see one girt with Urim and Thummim, precious stones, on which are written the twelve names of the tribes of Israel; we should behold him, crying unto his Father, "Forget not thy promises, forget not thy covenant;" we should hear him make mention of our sorrows, and tell forth our griefs on our behalf, for he is our intercessor. And could we behold the Father, we should not see him a listless and idle spectator of the intercession of the Son, but we should see him with attentive ear listening to every word of Jesus, and granting every petition. Where is the Holy Spirit all the while? Is he lying idle? O no; he is floating over the earth, and when he seas a weary soul, he says, "Come to Jesus, he will give you rest;" when he beholds an eye filled with tears, he wipes away the tears, and bids the mourner look for comfort on the cross; when he sees the tempest-tossed believer, he takes the helm of his soul and speaks the word of consolation; he helpeth the broken in heart, and bindeth up their wounds; and, ever on his mission of mercy, he flies around the world, being everywhere present. Behold, how the three persons work together. Do not then say, "I am grateful to the Son"—so you ought to be, but God the Son no more saves you than God the Father. Do not imagine that God the Father is a great tyrant, and that God the Son had to die to make him merciful. It was not to make the Father's love towards his people. Oh, no. One loves as much as the other; the three are conjoined in the great purpose of rescuing the elect from damnation.

But you must notice another thing in my text, which

will show the blessed unity of the three—the one person promises to the other. The Son says, "I will pray the Father." "Very well," the disciples may have said, "we can trust you for that." "And he will send you." You see, here is the Son signing a bond on behalf of the Father. "He will send you another Comforter." There is a bond on behalf of the Holy Spirit too. "And he will abide with you forever." One person speaks for the other, and how could they, if there were any disagreement between them? If one wished to save, and the other not, they could not promise on another's behalf. But whatever the Son says, the Father listens to; whatever the Father promises, the Holy Ghost works; and, whatever the Holy Ghost injects into the soul, that God the Father fulfils. So, the three together mutually promise on one another's behalf. There is a bond with three names appended—Father, Son, and Holy Ghost. By three immutable things, as well as by two, the Christian is secured beyond the reach of death and hell. A Trinity of securities, because there is a Trinity of God.

III. Our third point is, the *indwelling* of the Holy Ghost in believers. Now, beloved, these first two things have been matters of pure doctrine; this is the subject of experience. The indwelling of the Holy Ghost is a subject so profound, and so having to do with the inner man, that no soul will be able truly and really to comprehend what I say, unless it has been taught of God. I have heard of an old minister, who told a fellow of one of the Cambridge colleges, that he understood a language that *he* never learned in all his life. "I have not," he said, "even a smattering of Greek, and I know no Latin, but thank God, I can talk the language of Canaan, and that is more than you can." So, beloved, I shall now have to talk a little of the language of Canaan. If you cannot comprehend me, I am much afraid it is because you are not of Israelitish extraction; you are not a child of God, nor an inheritor of the kingdom of heaven.

We are told in the text, that Jesus would send the Comforter, who would abide in the saints forever; who would dwell with them, and be in them. Old Ignatius, the martyr, used to call himself Theophorus, or Godbearer, "because," said he, "I bear about with me the Holy Ghost." And truly every Christian is a Godbearer. "Know ye not that ye are the temples of the Holy Ghost? for he dwelleth in you?" That man is no Christian who is not the subject of the indwelling of the Holy Spirit; he may talk well, he may understand theology, and be a sound Calvinist; he will be the child of nature finely dressed, but not the living child. He may be a man of so profound an intellect, so gigantic a soul, so comprehensive a mind, and so lofty an imagination, that he may dive into all the secrets of nature, may know the path which the eagle's eye hath not seen, and go into depths where the ken of mortals reacheth not, but he shall not be a Christian with all his knowledge, he shall not be a son of God with all his researches, unless he understands what it is to have the Holy Ghost dwelling in him and abiding in him; yea, and that for ever.

Some people call this fanaticism, and they say, "You are a Quaker; why not follow George Fox?" Well, we would not mind that much: we would follow any one who followed the Holy Ghost. Even he, with all his eccentricities, I doubt not, was, in many cases, actually inspired by the Holy Spirit; and whenever I find a man in whom there rests the Spirit of God, the spirit within me leaps to hear the spirit within him, and we feel that we are one. The Spirit of God in one Christian soul recognizes the Spirit in another. I recollect talking with a good man, as I believe he was, who was insisting that it was impossible for us to know whether we had the Holy Spirit within us or not. I should like him to be here this morning, because I would read this verse to him, "But ye know him, for he dwelleth with you, and shall be in you." Ah! you think you cannot tell whether you have the Holy Spirit or not. Can I tell whether I am alive or not? If I were touched by electricity, could I tell whether I was or not? I suppose I should; the shock would be strong enough to make me know where I stood. So, if I have God within me—if I have Deity tabernacling in my breast—if I have God the Holy Ghost resting in my

heart, and making a temple of my body, do you think
I shall know it? Call it fanaticism if you will, but I trust
that there are some of us who know what it is to be
always, or generally, under the influence of the Holy
Spirit—always in one sense, generally in another. When
we have difficulties, we ask the direction of the Holy
Ghost. When we do not understand a portion of Holy
Scripture, we ask God the Holy Ghost to shine upon
us. When we are depressed, the Holy Ghost comforts
us. You cannot tell what the wondrous power of the
indwelling of the Holy Ghost is; how it pulls back the
hand of the saint when he would touch the forbidden
thing; how it prompts him to make a covenant with
his eyes; how it binds his feet, lest they should fall in
a slippery way; how it restrains his heart, and keeps
him from temptation. O ye, who know nothing of the
indwelling of the Holy Ghost, despise it not. O despise
not the Holy Ghost, for it is the unpardonable sin. "He
that speaketh a word against the Son of Man, it shall
be forgiven him, but he that speaketh against the Holy
Ghost, it shall never be forgiven him, either in this
life, or that which is to come." So saith the Word of
God. Therefore tremble, lest in anything ye despise the
influences of the Holy Spirit.

But before closing this point, there is one little word
that pleases me very much, that is "forever." You knew
I should not miss that; you were certain I could not let

it go without observation. "Abide with you forever." I wish I could get an Armenian here to finish my sermon. I fancy I see him taking that word "forever." He would say, "for—forever;" he would have to stammer and stutter; for he could never get it out all at once. He might stand and pull it about, and at last he would have to say, "The translation is wrong." And I suppose the poor man would have to prove that the original was wrong too. Ah! but blessed be God we can read it—"He shall abide with you forever." Once give me the Holy Ghost, and I shall never lose him till "forever" has run out; till eternity has spun its everlasting rounds.

IV. Now we have to close up with a brief remark on the reason why the world rejects the Holy Ghost. It is said, "Whom the world cannot receive, because it seeth him not, neither knoweth him." You know what is sometimes meant by "the world"—those whom God in his wondrous sovereignty passed over when he chose his people: the preterite ones; those passed over in God's wondrous preterition—not the reprobates who were condemned to damnation by some awful decree; but those passed over by God, when he chose out his elect. These cannot receive the Spirit. Again, it means all in a carnal state are not able to procure themselves this divine influence; and, thus it is true, "Whom the world cannot receive."

The unregenerate world of sinners despises the Holy Ghost, "because it seeth him not." Yes, I believe this is the great secret why many laugh at the idea of the existence of the Holy Ghost—because they see him not. You tell the worldling, "I have the Holy Ghost within me." He says, "I cannot see it." He wants it to be something tangible—a thing he can recognize with his senses. Have you ever heard the argument used by a good old Christian against an infidel doctor? The doctor said there was no soul, and asked, "Did you ever see a soul?" "No," said the Christian. "Did you ever hear a soul?" "No." "Did you ever smell a soul?" "No." "Did you ever taste a soul?" "No." "Did you ever feel a soul?" "Yes," said the man—"I feel I have one within me." "Well," said the doctor, "there are four senses against one; you only have one on your side." "Very well," said the Christian, "Did you ever see a pain?" "No." "Did you ever hear a pain?" "No." "Did you ever smell a pain?" "No." "Did you ever taste a pain?" "No." "Did you ever feel a pain?" "Yes." "And that is quite enough, I suppose, to prove there is a pain?" "Yes." So the worldling says there is no Holy Ghost, because he cannot see it. Well, but we feel it. You say that is fanaticism, and that we never felt it. Suppose you tell me that honey is bitter, I reply, "No, I am sure you cannot have tasted it; taste it and try." So with the Holy Ghost; if you did but feel his influence, you would no longer say there is no Holy Spirit, because you cannot see it. Are there not many things, even in nature, which we cannot see? Did you ever see the wind? No; but ye know there is wind, when you behold the hurricane tossing the waves about, and rending down the habitations of men; or when, in the soft evening zephyr, it kisses the flowers, and maketh dew-drops hang in pearly coronets around the rose. Did ye ever see electricity? No; but ye know there is such a thing, for it travels along the wires for thousands of miles, and carries our messages; though you cannot see the thing itself, you know there is such a thing. So you must believe there is a Holy Ghost working in us, both to will and to do, even though it is beyond our senses.

But the last reason why worldly men laugh at the doctrine of the Holy Spirit, is, because they do not know it. If they know it by heartfelt experience and if they recognized its agency in the soul; if they had ever been touched by it; if they had been made to tremble under a sense of sin; if they had had their hearts melted, they would never have doubted the existence of the Holy Ghost.

And now, beloved, it says, "He dwelleth with you, and shall be in you." We will close up with that sweet recollection—the Holy Ghost dwells in all believers and shall be with them.

One word of comment and advice to the saints of God, and to sinners, and I have done. Saints of the Lord! ye have this morning heard that God the Holy Ghost is a person; ye have had it proved to your souls. What follows from this? Why, it followeth how earnest ye should be in prayer *to* the Holy Spirit, as well as *for* the Holy Spirit. Let me say that this is an inference that you should lift up your prayers to the Holy Ghost: that you should cry earnestly unto him; for he is able to do exceeding abundantly above all you can speak or think. See this mass of people. What is to convert it? See this crowd? Who is to make my influence permeate through the mass? You know this place now has a mighty influence, and, God blessing us, it will have an influence not only upon this city, but upon England at large; for we now employ the press as well as the pulpit; and certainly, I should say, before the close of the year, more than two hundred thousand of my productions will be scattered through the land—words uttered by my lips, or written by my pen. But how can this influence be rendered for good? How shall God's glory be promoted by it? Only by incessant prayer for the Holy Spirit; by constantly calling down the influence of the Holy Ghost upon us; we want him to rest upon every page that is printed, and upon every word that is uttered. Let us then be doubly earnest in pleading with the Holy Ghost, that he would come and own our labors; that the whole church at large may be revived thereby, and not ourselves only, but the whole world share in the benefit.

Then, to the ungodly, I have this one closing word to say. Ever be careful how you speak of the Holy Ghost. I do not know what the unpardonable sin is, and I do not think any man understands it; but it is something like this: "He that speaketh a word against the Holy Ghost, it shall never be forgiven him." I do not know what that means; but tread carefully! There is danger; there is a pit which our ignorance has covered by sand; tread carefully! you may be in it before the next hour. If there is any strife in your heart to-day, perhaps you will go to the ale-house and forget it. Perhaps there is some voice speaking in your soul, and you will put it away. I do not tell you will be resisting the Holy Ghost, and committing the unpardonable sin; but it is somewhere there. Be very careful. O, there is no crime on earth so black as the crime against the Holy Spirit! Ye may blaspheme the Father, and ye shall be damned for it, unless ye repent; ye may blaspheme the Son, and hell shall be your portion, unless ye are forgiven; but blaspheme the Holy Ghost, and thus saith the Lord: "There is no forgiveness, either in this world nor in the world which is to come." I cannot tell you what it is; I do no profess to understand it; but there it is. It is the danger signal; stop! man, stop! If thou has despised the Holy Spirit— if thou hast laughed at his revelations, and scorned what Christians call his influence, I beseech thee, stop! This morning seriously deliberate. Perhaps some of you have actually committed the unpardonable sin; stop! Let fear stop you; sit down. Do not drive on so rashly as you have done, Jehu! O slacken your reins! Thou who are such a profligate in sin—thou who hast uttered such hard words against the Trinity, stop! Ah! it makes us all stop. It makes us all draw up, and say, "Have I not perhaps so done?" Let us think of this; and let us not at any time stifle either with the words or the acts of God the Holy Ghost.

THE COMFORTER

A SERMON
(No. 5)

Delivered on Sabbath Evening, January 21th, 1855,
by the REV. C. H. Spurgeon
At New Park Street Chapel, Southwark,

"But the Comforter, which is the Holy Ghost, whom
the Father will send in my name, he shall teach you
all things and bring all things to your remembrance,
whatsoever I have said unto you."—John 14:26.

GOOD OLD Simeon called Jesus the consolation of
Israel; and so he was. Before his actual appearance, his
name was the Day-Star; cheering the darkness, and
prophetic of the rising sun. To him they looked with
the same hope which cheers the nightly watcher, when
from the lonely castle-top he sees the fairest of the stars,
and hails her as the usher of the morn. When he was on
earth, he must have been the consolation of all those
who were privileged to be his companions. We can
imagine how readily the disciples would run to Christ
to tell him of their griefs, and how sweetly, with that
matchless intonation of his voice, he would speak to
them, and bid their fears be gone. Like children, they
would consider him as their Father; and to him every

want, every groan, every sorrow, every agony, would at once be carried; and he, like a wise physician, had a balm for every wound; he had mingled a cordial for their every care; and readily did he dispense some mighty remedy to allay all the fever of their troubles. Oh! it must have been sweet to have lived with Christ. Surely sorrows were then but joys in masks, because they gave an opportunity to go to Jesus to have them removed. Oh! would to God, some of us may say, that we could have lain our weary heads upon the bosom of Jesus, and that our birth had been in that happy era, when we might have heard his kind voice, and seen his kind look, when he said, "Let the weary ones come unto me."

But now he was about to die. Great prophecies were to be fulfilled; and great purposes were to be answered; and therefore Jesus must go. It behoved him to suffer, that he might be made a propitiation for our sins. It behoved him to slumber in the dust awhile, that he might perfume the chamber of the grave to make it—

"No more a charnel house to fence
The relics of lost innocence."

It behoved him to have a resurrection, that we, who shall one day be the dead in Christ, might rise first, and in glorious bodies stand upon earth. And if behoved him that he should ascend up on high, that he might lead captivity captive; that he might chain the fiends of hell; that he might lash them to his chariot wheels, and drag them up high heaven's hill, to make them feel a second overthrow from his right arm, when he should dash them from the pinnacles of heaven down to the deeper depths beneath. "It is right I should go away from you," said Jesus, "for if I go not away, the Comforter will not come." Jesus must go. Weep, ye disciples; Jesus must be gone. Mourn, ye poor ones, who are to be left without a Comforter. But hear how kindly Jesus speaks: "I will not leave you comfortless, I will pray the Father, and he shall send you another Comforter, who shall be with you, and shall dwell in you forever." He would not leave those few poor sheep alone in the wilderness; he would not desert his children, and leave them fatherless. Albeit that he had a mighty mission which did fill his heart and hand; albeit he had so much to perform, that we might have thought that even his gigantic intellect would be overburdened; albeit he had so much to suffer, that we might suppose his whole soul to be concentrated upon the thought of the sufferings to be endured. Yet it was not so; before he left, he gave soothing words of comfort; like the good Samaritan, he poured in oil and wine, and we see what he promised: "I will send you another Comforter—one who shall be just what I have been, yea, even more; who shall console you in your sorrows, remove your doubts, comfort you in your afflictions, and stand as my vicar on earth, to do that which I would have done had I tarried with you."

Before I discourse of the Holy Ghost as the Comforter, I must make one or two remarks on the different translations of the word rendered "Comforter." The Rhenish translation, which you are aware is adopted by Roman Catholics, has left the word untranslated, and gives it "Paraclete." "But the Paraclete, which is the Holy Ghost, whom the Father will send in my name, he shall teach you all things." This is the original Greek word, and it has some other meanings besides "Comforter." Sometimes it means the monitor or instructor: "I will send you another monitor, another teacher." Frequently it means "Advocate;" but the most common meaning of the word is that which we have here: "I will send you another *Comforter*." However, we cannot pass over those other two interpretations without saying something upon them.

"I will send you another *teacher*." Jesus Christ had been the official teacher of his saints whilst on earth. They called no man Rabbi except Christ. They sat at no men's feet to learn their doctrines; but they had them direct from the lips of him who "spake as never man spake." "And now," says he, "when I am gone, where shall you find the great infallible teacher? Shall I set you up a pope at Rome, to whom you shall go, and who shall be your infallible oracle? Shall I give you the councils of the church to be held to decide all knotty points?" Christ said no such thing. "I am the infallible paraclete, or teacher, and when I am gone, I will send you another teacher, and he shall be the person who is to explain Scripture; he shall be the authoritative oracle of God, who shall make all dark things light, who shall unravel mysteries, who shall untwist all knots of revelation, and shall make you understand what you could not discover, had it not been for his influence." And, beloved, no man ever learns anything aright, unless he is taught of the Spirit. You may learn election, and you may know it so that you shall be damned by it, if you are not taught of the Holy Ghost; for I have known some who have learned election to their soul's destruction; they have learned it so that they said they were of the elect, whereas, they had no marks, no evidences, and no works of the Holy Ghost in their souls. There is a way of learning truth in Satan's college, and holding it in licentiousness; but if so, it shall be to your souls as poison to your veins and prove your everlasting ruin. No man can know Jesus Christ unless he is taught of God. There is no doctrine of the Bible which can be safely, thoroughly, and truly learned, except by the agency of the one authoritative teacher. Ah! tell me not of systems of divinity; tell me not of schemes of theology; tell me not of infallible commentators, or most learned and most arrogant doctors; but tell me of the Great Teacher, who shall instruct us, the sons of God, and shall make us wise to understand all things. He is *the* Teacher; it matters not what this man or that man says; I rest on no man's boasting authority, nor will you. Ye are not to be carried away with the craftiness of men, nor sleight of words; this is the authoritative oracle—the Holy Ghost resting in the hearts of his children.

The other translation is *advocate*. Have you ever thought how the Holy Ghost can be said to be an advocate? You know Jesus Christ is called the wonderful, the counsellor, the mighty God; but how can the Holy Ghost be said to be an advocate? I suppose it is thus; he is an advocate on earth to plead against the enemies of the cross. How was it that Paul could so ably plead before Felix and Agrippa? How was it that the Apostles stood unawed before the magistrates, and confessed their Lord? How has it come to pass, that in all times God's ministers have been made fearless as lions, and their brows have been firmer than brass; their hearts sterner than steel, and their words like the language of God? Why, it was simply for this reason; that it was not the man who pleaded, but it was God the Holy Ghost pleading through him. Have you never seen an earnest minister, with hands uplifted and eyes dropping tears, pleading with the sons of men? Have you never admired that portrait from the hand of old John Bunyan?—a grave person with eyes lifted up to heaven, the best of books in his hand, the law of truth written on his lips, the world behind his back, standing as if he pleaded with men, and a crown of gold hanging over his head. Who gave that minister so blessed a manner, and such goodly matter? Whence came his skill? Did he acquire it in the college? Did he learn it in the seminary? Ah, no. He learned it of the God of Jacob; he learned it of the Holy Ghost; for the Holy Ghost is the great counsellor who teaches us how to advocate his cause aright.

But, beside this, the Holy Ghost is the advocate in men's hearts. Ah! I have known men reject a doctrine until the Holy Ghost began to illuminate them. We, who are the advocates of the truth, are often very poor pleaders; we spoil our cause by the words we use; but it is a mercy that the brief is in the hand of a special pleader, who will advocate successfully, and overcome the sinner's opposition. Did you ever know him fail once? Brethren, I speak to your souls; has not God in old times convinced you of sin? Did not the Holy Ghost come and prove that you were guilty, although no minister could ever get you out of your self-righteousness? Did he not advocate Christ's righteousness? Did he not stand and tell you that your works were filthy rags? And when you had well-nigh still refused to listen to his voice, did he not fetch hell's drum and make it sound about your ears; bidding you look through the vista of future years, and see the throne set, and the books open, and the sword brandished, and hell burning, and fiends howling, and the damned shrieking forever? And did he not convince you of the judgment to come? He is a mighty advocate when he pleads in the soul—of sin, of righteousness, and of the judgment to come. Blessed advocate! Plead in my heart; plead with my conscience. When I sin, make conscience bold to tell me of it; when I err, make conscience speak at once; and when I turn aside to crooked ways, then advocate the cause of righteousness, and bid me sit down in confusion, knowing by guiltiness in the sight of God.

But there is yet another sense in which the Holy Ghost advocates, and that is, he advocates our cause with Jesus Christ, with groanings that cannot be uttered. O my soul! thou art ready to burst within me. O my heart! thou art swelled with grief. The hot tide of my emotion would well-nigh overflood the channels of my veins. I long to speak, but the very desire chains my tongue. I wish to pray, but the fervency of my feeling curbs my language. There is a groaning within that cannot be uttered. Do you know who can utter that groaning? who can understand it, and who can put it into heavenly language, and utter it in a celestial tongue, so that Christ can hear it? O yes; it is God the Holy Spirit; he advocates our cause with Christ, and then Christ advocates it with his Father. He is the advocate who maketh intercession for us, with groanings that cannot be uttered.

Having thus explained the Spirit's office as a teacher and advocate, we now come to the translation of our version—the *Comforter*; and here I shall have three divisions: first, the *comforter*; secondly, the *comfort*; and thirdly, the *comforted*.

I. First, then, the COMFORTER. Briefly let me run over in my mind, and in your minds too, the characteristics of this glorious Comforter. Let me tell you some of the attributes of his comfort, so that you may understand how well adapted he is to your case.

And first, we will remark, that God the Holy Ghost is a very *loving* Comforter. I am in distress, and I want consolation. Some passer-by hears of my sorrow, and he steps within, sits down, and essays to cheer me; he speaks soothing words, but he loves me not; he is a stranger; he knows me not at all; he has only come in to try his skill. And what is the consequence? His words run o'er me like oil upon a slab of marble—they are like the pattering rain upon the rock; they do not break my grief; it stands unmoved as adamant, because he has no love for me. But let some one who loves me dear as his own life, come and plead with me, then truly his words are music; they taste like honey; he knows the password of the doors of my heart, and my ear is attentive to every word; I catch the intonation of each syllable as it falls, for it is like the harmony of the harps of heaven.

Oh! there is a voice in love, it speaks a language which is its own; it has an idiom and a brogue which none can mimic; wisdom cannot imitate it; oratory cannot attain unto it; it is love alone which can reach the mourning heart; love is the only handkerchief which can wipe the mourner's tears away. And is not the Holy Ghost a loving comforter? Dost thou know, O saint, how much the Holy Spirit loves thee? Canst thou measure the love of the Spirit? Dost thou know how great is the affection of his soul towards thee? Go measure heaven with thy span; go weigh the mountains in the scales; go take the ocean's water, and tell each drop; go count the sand upon the sea's wide shore; and when thou hast accomplished this, thou canst tell how much he loveth thee. He has loved thee long, he has loved thee well, he loved thee ever, and he still shall love thee; surely he is the person to comfort thee, because he loves. Admit him, then, to your heart, O Christian, that he may comfort you in your distress.

But next, he is a *faithful* Comforter. Love sometimes proveth unfaithful. "Oh! sharper than a serpent's tooth" is an unfaithful friend! Oh! far more bitter than the gall of bitterness, to have a friend turn from me in my distress! Oh! woe of woes, to have one who loves me in my prosperity, forsake me in the dark day of my trouble. Sad indeed; but such is not God's Spirit. He ever loves, and loves even to the end—a faithful Comforter. Child of God, you are in trouble. A little while ago, you found him a sweet and loving Comforter; you obtained relief from him when others were but broken cisterns; he sheltered you in his bosom, and carried you in his arms. Oh, wherefore dost thou distrust him now? Away with thy fears; for he is a faithful Comforter. "Ah! but," thou sayest, "I fear I shall be sick, and shall be deprived of his ordinances." Nevertheless he shall visit thee on thy sick bed, and sit by thy side, to give thee consolation. "Ah! but I have distresses greater than you can conceive of; wave upon wave rolleth over me; deep calleth unto deep, at the noise of the Eternal's waterspouts." Nevertheless, he will be faithful to his promise. "Ah! but I have sinned." So thou hast, but sin cannot sever thee from his love; he loves thee still. Think not, O poor downcast child of God, because the scars of thine old sins have marred thy beauty, that he loves thee less because of that blemish. O no! He loved thee when he foreknew thy sin; he loved thee with the knowledge of what the aggregate of thy wickedness would be; and he does not love thee less now. Come to him in all boldness of faith; tell him thou hast grieved him, and he will forget thy wandering, and will receive thee again; the kisses of his love shall be bestowed upon thee, and the arms of his grace shall embrace thee. He is faithful; trust him, he will never deceive you; trust him, he will never leave you.

Again, he is an *unwearied* Comforter. I have sometimes tried to comfort persons, and have been tired. You, now and then, meet with a case of a nervous person. You ask, "What is your trouble?" You are told; and you essay, if possible, to remove it; but while you are preparing your artillery to battle the trouble, you find that it has shifted its quarters, and is occupying quite a different position. You change your argument and begin again; but lo, it is again gone, and you are bewildered. You feel like Hurcules, cutting off the evergrowing heads of the Hydra, and you give up your task in despair. You meet with persons whom it is impossible to comfort, reminding one of the man who locked himself up in fetters, and threw the key away, so that nobody could unlock him. I have found some in the fetters of despair. "O, I am the man," say they, "that has seen affliction; pity me, pity me, O, my friends;" and the more you try to comfort such people, the worse they get; and, therefore, out of all heart, we leave them to wander alone among the tombs of their former joys. But the Holy Ghost is never out of heart with those whom he wishes to comfort. He attempts to comfort us, and we run away from the sweet cordial; he gives us some sweet draught to cure us, and we will not drink it; he gives some wondrous potion to charm away all our troubles, and we put it away from us. Still be pursues us; and though we say that we will not be comforted, he says we *shall* be, and when he has said, he does it; he is not to be wearied by all our sins, nor by all our murmurings.

And oh, how *wise* a Comforter is the Holy Ghost. Job had comforters, and I think he spoke the truth when he said, "Miserable comforters are ye all." But I dare say they esteemed themselves wise; and when the young man Elihu rose to speak, they thought he had a world of impudence. Were they not "grave and reverend seigniors?" Did not they comprehend his grief and sorrow? If they could not comfort him, who could? But they did not find out the cause. They thought he was not really a child of God, that he was self-righteous, and they gave him the wrong physic. It is a bad case when the doctor mistakes a disease and gives a wrong prescription, and so perhaps kills the patient. Sometimes, when we go and visit people, we mistake their disease; we want to comfort them on this point, whereas they do not require any such comfort at all, and they would be better left alone, than spoiled by such unwise comforters as we are. But oh, how wise the Holy Spirit is! He takes the soul, lays it on the table, and dissects it in a moment; he finds out the root of the matter, he sees where the complaint is, and then he applies the knife where something is required to be taken away, or puts a plaster where the sore is; and he never mistakes. O how wise is the blessed Holy Ghost; from ever comforter I turn, and leave them all, for thou art he who alone givest the wisest consolation.

Then mark, how *safe* a Comforter the Holy Ghost is. All comfort is not safe, mark that. There is a young man over there very melancholy. You know how he became so. He stepped into the house of God and heard a powerful preacher, and the word was blessed, and convinced him of sin. When he went home, his father and the rest found there was something different about him, "Oh," they said, "John is mad, he is crazy;" and what said his mother? "Send him into the country for a week; let him go to the ball or the theatre." John, did you find any comfort there? "Ah no; they made me worse, for while I was there I thought hell might open and swallow me up." Did you find any relief in the gayeties of the world? "No," say you, "I thought it was idle waste of time." Alas! this is miserable comfort, but it is the comfort of the worldling; and, when a Christian gets into distress, how many will recommend him this remedy and the other. "Go and hear Mr. So-and-so preach;" "have a few friends at you house;" "Read such-and-such a consoling volume;" and very likely it is the most unsafe advice in the world. The devil will sometimes come to men's souls as a false comforter; and he will say to the soul, "What need is there to make all this ado about repentance? you are no worse than other people;" and he will try to make the soul believe, that what is presumption, is the real assurance of the Holy Ghost; thus he deceives many by false comfort. Ah! there have been many, like infants, destroyed by elixirs, given to lull them to sleep; many have been ruined by the cry of "peace, peace," when there is no peace; hearing gentle things, when they ought to be stirred to the quick. Cleopatra's asp was brought in a basket of flowers; and men's ruin often lurks in fair and sweet speeches. But the Holy Ghost's comfort is safe, and you may rest on it. Let him speak the word, and there is a reality about it; let him give the cup of consolation, and you may drink it to the bottom; for in its depths there are no dregs, nothing to intoxicate or ruin, it is all safe.

Moreover, the Holy Ghost is an *active* Comforter; he does not comfort by words, but by deeds. Some comfort by, "Be ye warmed, and be ye filled, giving nothing." But the Holy Ghost gives, he intercedes with Jesus; he gives us promises, he gives us grace, and so he comforts us. Mark again, he is always a *successful* Comforter; he never attempts what he cannot accomplish.

Then, to close up, he is an *ever-present* Comforter, so that you never have to send for him. Your God is always near you; and when you need comfort in your distress, behold the word is nigh thee; it is in thy mouth, and in thy heart. He is an ever-present help in time of trouble. I wish I had time to expand these thoughts, but I cannot.

II. The second thing is the COMFORT. Now there

are some persons who make a great mistake about the influence of the Holy Spirit. A foolish man, who had a fancy to preach in a certain pulpit, though in truth he was quite incapable of the duty, called upon the minister, and assured him solemnly, that it had been revealed to him by the Holy Ghost that he was to preach in his pulpit. "Very well," said the minister, "I suppose I must not doubt your assertion, but as it has not been revealed to me that I am to let you preach, you must go your way, until it is." I have heard many fanatical persons say the Holy Spirit revealed this and that to them. Now, that is very generally revealed nonsense. The Holy Ghost does not reveal anything fresh now. He brings old things to our remembrance. "He shall teach you all things, and bring all things to your remembrance, whatsoever I have told you." The canon of revelation is closed, there is no more to be added; God does not give a fresh revelation, but he rivets the old one. When it has been forgotten, and laid in the dusty chamber of our memory, he fetches it out and cleans the picture, but does not paint a new one. There are no new doctrines, but the old ones are often revived. It is not, I say, by any new revelation that the Spirit comforts. He does so by telling us old things over again; he brings a fresh lamp to manifest the treasures hidden in Scripture; he unlocks the strong chests in which the truth has long lain, and he points to secret chamber filled with untold riches; but he coins no more, for enough is done. Believer! there is enough in the Bible for thee to live upon forever. If thou shouldst outnumber the years of Methuselah, there would be no need for a fresh revelation; if thou shouldst live till Christ should come upon the earth, there would be no need for the addition of a single word; if thou shouldst go down as deep as Jonah, or even descend as David said he did into the belly of hell, still there would be enough in the Bible to comfort thee without a supplementary sentence. But Christ says, "He shall take of mine, and show it unto you." Now, let me just tell you briefly what it is the Holy Ghost tells us.

Ah! does he not whisper to the heart, "Saint, be of good cheer; there is one who died for thee; look to Calvary, behold his wounds, see the torrent gushing from his side—there is thy purchaser, and thou art secure. He loves thee with an everlasting love, and this chastisement is meant for thy good; each stroke is working thy healing; by the blueness of the wound thy soul is made better." "Whom he loveth he chasteneth, and scourgeth every son whom he receiveth." Doubt not his grace, because of thy tribulation; but believe that he loveth thee as much in seasons of trouble, as in times of happiness. And then, moreover, he says, "What is all thy suffering compared with that of thy Lord's? or what, when weighed in the scales of Jesus' agonies, is all thy distress? And especially at times does the Holy Ghost take back the veil of heaven, and lets the soul behold the glory of the upperworld! Then it is that the saint can say, "O thou art a Comforter to me!"

> "Let cares like a wild deluge come,
>   And storms of sorrow fall;
> May I but safely reach my home,
>   My God, my heaven, my all."

Some of you could follow, were I to tell of manifestations of heaven. You, too, have left sun, moon, and stars at your feet, while, in you flight, outstripping the tardy lightning, you have seemed to enter the gates of pearl, and tread the golden streets, borne aloft on wings of the Spirit. But here we must not trust ourselves; lest, lost in reverie, we forget our theme.

III. And now, thirdly, who are the comforted persons? I like, you know, at the end of my sermon to cry out, "Divide! divide!" There are two parties here—some who are comforted, and others who are the comfortless ones—some who have received the consolations of the Holy Ghost, and some who have not. Now let us try and sift you, and see which is the chaff and which is the wheat; and may God grant that some of the chaff may, this night, be transformed into his wheat!

You may say, "How am I to know whether I am a recipient of the comfort of the Holy Ghost?" You may know it by one rule. If you have received one blessing from God, you will receive all other blessings too. Let me explain myself. If I could come here as an auctioneer, and sell the gospel off in lots, I should dispose of it all. If I could say, here is justification through the blood of Christ—free; giving away, gratis; many a one would say, "I will have justification; give it to me; I wish to be justified; I wish to be pardoned." Suppose I took sanctification, the giving up of all sin, a thorough change of heart, leaving off drunkenness and swearing; many would say, "I don't want that; I should like to go to heaven, but I do not want that holiness; I should like to be saved at last, but I should like to have my drink still; I should like to enter glory, but then I must have an oath or two on the road." Nay, but, sinner, if thou hast one blessing, thou shalt have all. God will never divide the gospel. He will not give justification to that man, and sanctification to another—pardon to one, and holiness to another. No, it all goes together. Whom he call, them he justifies; whom he justifies, them he sanctifies; and whom he sanctifies, them he also glorifies. Oh; if I could lay down nothing but the *comforts* of the gospel, ye would fly to them as flies do to honey. When ye come to be ill, ye send for the clergyman. Ah! you all want your minister then to come and give you consoling words. But, if he be an honest man, he will not give some of you a particle of consolation. He will not commence pouring oil, when the knife would be better. I want to make a man feel his sins before I dare tell him anything about Christ. I want to probe into his soul and make him feel that he is lost before I tell him anything about the purchased blessing. It is the ruin of many to tell them, "Now just believe on Christ, and that is all you have to do." If, instead of dying, they get better, they rise up white-washed hypocrites—that is all. I have heard of a city missionary who kept a record of two thousand persons who were supposed to be on their death-bed, but recovered, and whom he should have put down as converted persons had they died; and how many do you think lived a Christian life afterwards out of the two thousand? Not two. Positively he could only find one who was found to live afterwards in the fear of God. Is it not horrible that when men and women come to die, they should cry, "Comfort, comfort?" and that hence their friends conclude that they are children of God, while, after all, they have no right to consolation, but are intruders upon the enclosed grounds of the blessed God. O God, may these people ever be kept from having comfort when they have no right to it! Have you the other blessings? Have you had the conviction of sin? Have you ever felt your guilt before God? Have your souls been humbled at Jesus' feet? And have you been made to look to Calvary alone for your refuge? If not, you have no right to consolation. Do not take an atom of it. The Spirit is a convincer before he is a Comforter; and you must have the other operations of the Holy

Spirit, before you can derive anything from this.

And now I have done. You have heard what this babbler hath said once more. What has it been? Something about the Comforter. But let me ask you, before you go, what do you know about the Comforter? Each one of you, before descending the steps of this chapel, let this solemn question thrill through your souls—What do you know of the Comforter? O! poor souls, if ye know not the Comforter, I will tell you what you shall know—You shall know the Judge! If ye know not the Comforter on earth, ye shall know the Condemner in the next world, who shall cry, "Depart, ye cursed, into everlasting fire in hell." Well might Whitefield call out, "O earth, earth, earth, hear the word of the Lord!" If ye were to live here forever, ye might slight the gospel; if ye had a lease of your lives, ye might despise the Comforter. But, sirs, ye must die. Since last we met together, probably some have gone to their long last home; and ere we meet again in this sanctuary, some here will be amongst the glorified above, or amongst the damned below. Which will it be? Let you soul answer. If to-night you fell down dead in your pews, or where you are standing in the gallery, where would you be? in *heaven* or in *hell*? Ah! deceive not yourselves; let conscience have its perfect work; and if in the sight of God, you are obliged to say, "I tremble and fear lest my portion should be with unbelievers," listen one moment, and then I have done with thee. "He that believeth and is baptized shall be saved, and he that believeth not shall be damned." Weary sinner, hellish sinner, thou who art the devil's castaway, reprobate, profligate, harlot, robber, thief, adulterer, fornicator, drunkard, swearer, Sabbath-breaker—list! I speak to thee as well as to the rest. I exempt no man. God hath said there is no exemption here. "*Whosoever* believeth on the name of Jesus Christ shall be saved." Sin is no barrier; thy guilt is no obstacle. Whosoever—though he were as black as Satan, though he were filthy as a fiend—whosoever this night believes, shall have every sin forgiven, shall have every crime effaced; shall have ever iniquity blotted out; shall be saved in the Lord Jesus Christ, and shall stand in heaven safe and secure. That is the glorious gospel. God apply it to your hearts, and give you faith in Jesus!

"We have listened to the preacher—
Truth by him has now been shown;
But we want a GREATER TEACHER,
From the everlasting throne;
APPLICATION
Is the work of God alone."